SPEAKING OF STENDHAL

SPEAKING OF STENDHAL

by

STORM JAMESON

LONDON
VICTOR GOLLANCZ LTD
1979

© Storm Jameson 1975

ISBN 0 575 02571 9

Printed in Great Britain at
The Camelot Press Ltd, Southampton

✝

7015506

For G. C.
semper ubique vale

Preface

THIS IS NOT an attempt at a full-length historical study of the man whose reticence about his deep emotions misled intimate friends, and has teased the curiosity of a century and a half. Not only is there very little need for another biography of him—a huge number of works, critical and biographical, exist in France and some few in English—but I have not world enough, nor time, left me to attempt one. At most I have only time to speak about him as one speaks in suitable company of a friend.

The friend one makes for life at eighteen is not the person one knows at fifty-eight, sixty-eight, seventy-eight. When one has lived for the better part of a lifetime with a dead writer it is difficult to disengage him from the changing image, formed slowly and added to almost without intention, which has come to figure in the mind more clearly than the man as he figures in the documents, including his journals, letters, autobiographical works, and in the records of his contemporaries. Not a wholly false image, but differing in countless ways from those images formed by other readers, and as radically as all these differ from the idea the man had of himself. All are more or less the truth, as far as it can be known, except to God.

Great writers of any epoch can be divided into two kinds, the self-destroyers, a Balzac, a Byron, and the self-preservers, the Goethes. Is it only because he belongs indisputably with the first that Henri Beyle—he was over thirty when as a writer he became Stendhal—still seduces generation after generation of readers? No one would smile more quizzically than he to see himself the centre of a cult, his letters and scrawled notes deciphered, his views, motives, quips, analysed, his travels mapped, his briefest infatuation spied on, his steps followed from salon to salon, lodging to lodging. No writer has been more mercilessly dissected. We

7

know more about his activities than did his friends. But do we know him better than they did?

That old Paul Léautaud, himself a monster of repressed sensibility, writing in 1901, said: 'Chez Stendhal, l'homme est si particulier, qu'il n'y a pas de milieu: on l'adore ou on le déteste.' He was little given to adoration, but he and Stendhal had a living nerve in common, an unappeased longing for tenderness: it started, I dare say, at the same depth in both; Léautaud's mother lightheartedly abandoned her infant, Stendhal's died when he was seven.

He never aged: the born rebel, the child who, alone of his right-thinking family, was heart and soul for the Republic, who rejoiced when Louis XVI was guillotined, and loathed with an equal rage Jesuits and a purse-proud middle class, the adolescent determined to become the new Molière, the mocker at self-important authority, survived unchanged in the man dying at fifty-nine. At least one of the reasons why he continues to seduce. The man and the work are inalienably one: his heart beats in it. 'Il n'est pas une phrase parfaite de M. Anatole France qui donne autant d'émotion que la moindre phrase sèche, écrite sans souci, de ce tendre et troublant Stendhal.' Léautaud again. He prided himself on being guided by what, drawing the word out, he called *la lo-gique*. But as Mérimée pointed out in the slightly ambivalent memoir he wrote of his friend and published eight years after Stendhal's death: 'Toute sa vie il fut dominé par son imagination et ne fit rien que brusquement et d'enthousiasme. Cependant il se piquait de n'agir jamais que conformément à la raison. "Il faut en tout se guider par la LO-GIQUE," disait-il en mettant un intervalle entre la première syllabe et le reste du mot. Mais il souffrait impatiemment que la logique des autres ne fût pas la sienne.' There was indeed nothing mathematical about his logic. It was purely a question of style, of his passion for lucidity and a dry accuracy. He was a volcano of enthusiasms and prejudices, and recklessly imprudent in talk. Recalling when he was fifty-two that at the age of nine he had been rebuked, by the tutor he hated, for saying what he felt, he reflected that if the lesson had taken he would have become rich and a scoundrel. He was never in danger of it. Throughout a career which was not, except for a short time, at the most eight years, easy, he took little trouble to ingratiate himself in the right quarters: if it involved him in making friends with a bore, never. I doubt he ever lifted a finger to cultivate an important man for no better reason than that the fellow might be useful to him: 'Le seul malheur est de mener une vie ennuyeuse.' And since a successful career in any intellectual field rests for at least two-thirds on a willingness to be bored it is no wonder that his more influential friends came to feel that he was not a man it would be wise to help towards any very important position; he was too unreliable, too erratic, not devoutly enough interested in getting on, and emphatic in the wrong way about the wrong things. In short, a dear fellow, but not sound.

One of the more extraordinary things about this extraordinary man is that he knew where to lay the blame for his lack of success. 'Ce qui marque ma différence avec les niais importants du journal et *qui portent leur tête comme un saint-sacrement*, c'est que je n'ai jamais cru que la société me dût la moindre chose. Helvétius me sauva de cette énorme sottise. *La société paye les services qu'elle voit.* . . . Je n'ai donc jamais eu l'idée que les hommes fussent injustes envers moi.'

I am prepared to think that the coolness of this degree of self-knowledge unlocks one of the paradoxes which make it difficult to fathom him. Why has he, so much written about and pursued, had no or almost no influence on later writers? Why, rather than an influence, is he a cult? It is not simply that he is inimitable. The same must be said of Joyce and Proust, which has not kept back a ragged mob of Joycean and Proustifying novelists. Is it because there is something humbling about a man who under cover of a reckless frankness withheld his inmost self? Or is it because the man revealed in his letters, diaries, journals, in the superb *Vie de Henry Brulard* and in the *Souvenirs d'égotisme* exercises so powerful a fascination that interest about him has been largely channelled into curiosity about his life, every reachable cranny of which has been explored? I don't know. The fact remains that a novelist can be

9

soaked in his work, as Jean Dutourd is, without his own novels showing any trace of the master's influence. The obvious apparent exception, Jean Giono in certain of his later novels, is evidence that no one can be influenced by Stendhal by wishing to be—large stretches of Giono's novels about Angelo, from *Le Hussard sur le toit* onward, read like pastiche, not always very subtle pastiche either. Perhaps Giuseppe di Lampedusa's one novel, *Il Gattopardo*, is the single work which would not have been what it is but for its author's feeling for Stendhal. A writer can be influenced by a predecessor—except in essentially superficial ways—only if he is capable of responding at a great depth to the intimate movement of the older writer's mind, only if, as a writer, he shares the same blood type. I suspect that the possibility of a successful transfusion is much rarer than is generally allowed. Or that certain great writers, Stendhal one of them, have so rare an intellectual and spiritual blood type that it cannot be accepted by any but the one man in a million who has the same type in his writer's veins. Lampedusa is perhaps the only novelist who can be said to have been deeply and subtly influenced by Stendhal.

I regret hardly at all that I have left it too late to write the long book I hoped, many years ago, to attempt. The most indefatigable of Stendhal's biographers, M. Henri Martineau, can have overlooked few details. And one critical work, *La création chez Stendhal*, by Jean Prévost, will not mislead you by a thought's span. After that, all you need do is read and re-read Stendhal himself. Over the years I have read everything available to me, and before allowing myself this essay have re-read all that has been gathered together of his correspondence—and for good measure Mérimée's—and I know that such knowledge as I have of him comes from his own work.

SPEAKING OF STENDHAL

Chapter 1

MARIE-HENRI BEYLE was born in Grenoble in a tall gloomy house in the rue des Vieux-Jésuites on 23 January 1783. On his father's side he sprang from hard Dauphinois stock, with deeply-sunk peasant roots in the Vercors: his great-great-grandfather was a prosperous draper in Lans-en-Vercors whose immediate descendants moved out of trade to become government servants, lawyers, magistrates, landed gentry. He preferred to think of himself as belonging to his mother's more cultivated family, the Gagnons: these came from Provence, and there was a strong tradition in the family that they were remotely Italian in origin. He liked to believe it. For his father he felt, already as a child, only dislike and an involuntary physical repugnance. Never, he wrote in his fifties, had chance brought together two more radically antipathetic human beings. The antipathy is real enough, but, unlike as they were in every other respect, there was a deeply buried likeness; it was from his father that he had his emotional vulnerability and the instinctive mistrust with which he hid it. A circumstance that ironically separated them; they never came within speaking distance of each other.

Seen through his young son's eyes, Chérubin Beyle was without graces of mind or body. He was pock-marked and unattractive, avaricious, dour, straitlaced, interested only in making money; in short, *archi-Dauphinois*. No doubt an exact portrait. But try hanging it in another light. Left when he was seventeen the head of his family, with ten sisters on his hands, he set to work with native courage, and after some fourteen or fifteen years of desperately hard work had become a successful barrister, with a position in the High Court of Grenoble. Now at thirty-four he could think of marriage, and he married Henriette Gagnon, ten years younger, the daughter of one of the more highly respected citizens of Grenoble, a fashionable doctor able to give her a dowry of twenty thousand francs. Chérubin Beyle had every right to hope and did hope and intend to advance himself and his children, socially as well as financially. There was a flaw in his plans, but who, at this point, could have supposed that he would both father a prodigy of self-will and genius and ruin himself in his speculative efforts to climb still higher.

His young wife was a lively pretty creature, cultivated, reading Dante in the original, quick-witted, gay. Her son was, he insists, passionately in love with her, wanting to cover her body with kisses, detesting his father when he came between them. Very like any sensuously lively male infant. When she died in childbirth he was seven years old. He endured all a child's violent unmanageable despair. His life changed completely. His father became more silent, more rigid, more morose, and austerely pious: there were few visitors to the house except priests, and no conversation except about money. Dying, his mother had asked her unmarried sister to look after him and his two sisters, Pauline aged four, and the two-year-old Zénaïde. Séraphie Gagnon was thirty, but he always speaks of her as a sour old maid, delighted when she could convict him of misbehaviour and have him punished. This female devil, as he calls her, darkened his childhood. There were violent scenes. No doubt he made himself as troublesome as will any spirited child who feels himself unliked and thwarted, and no doubt, though not a devil, she handled him badly, a child craving to be loved and admired. She seems never to have liked him, even before he became her responsibility. He was not more than three when she declared that he was a monster, with an atrocious character— instead of kissing a woman visitor's heavily rouged cheek he had bitten it—and a year later accused him of deliberately trying to kill another woman by dropping a knife on her from an upper window.

In later life he was prepared to believe that the harshness and incomprehension that turned an eager affectionate little boy into a sullen rebel had saved him from becoming a tame conformist. It is remotely possible. Naturally he rejected his father's and Séraphie's right-thinking creeds; they were his enemies, the enemies of the 'pauvre petit bambin persécuté' he calls himself. But the ten-year-old, 'seized by one of the sharpest impulses of joy' he had ever felt in his life when he heard that Louis XVI had been guillotined, was born a rebel against authority of any kind. He could have been gentled, steadied, but not, not deeply, changed.

Had he been confined to a house from which all gaiety and tenderness had disappeared he would have been poorly off, but he was not. The warmth and gentleness he was deprived of at home he found not more than a hundred yards away, in his mother's father's house facing the sunny place Grenette and the Grande-Rue: here were wide rooms and at the second-floor level a terrace with a superb view to mountains where on warm evenings his grandfather talked to him intelligently and gaily, and as the summer darkness fell taught him to name the stars. Dr Gagnon was a very civilised old gentleman, an admirer of Voltaire whose bust he kept on his writing desk, a prudent tolerant liberal, disliking extremism whether in politics or emotions, capable of tenderness, capable of protesting an injustice, but not beyond the point of danger: during the Terror he held his tongue, and between discretion and his fellow-citizens' respect and liking for him was never disturbed. He was interested in science and medical administration; he had a genuine passion for education, and spent time, energy and his own money to help create the Grenoble public library. To say that he formed Henri is something of a pious exaggeration—the material was both volatile and not exactly malleable—but certainly he gave the child the assurance he desperately needed of being loved, and wakened in him an enduring passion to *learn*, in a sense not in the Beyle vocabulary. He did more than this. If he did not form his grandson's manner of life he formed his literary style. In the Gagnon family slovenly speech was severely frowned on or unsparingly mocked. The boy learned early to use 'the simplest phrasing and the most precise word'. What supreme luck, less perhaps for him—he would have been more admired as a writer by his contemporaries if he had been less fastidiously direct and lucid—than for his future readers, for us.

The second member of the family, Dr Gagnon's unmarried sister, thin, inflexible, nine years his senior, was as civilised, as delicately indulgent of a highly-strung child, and in her own way talked to him with as much human respect. More austere, morally more rigid than her brother, Élizabeth Gagnon infected with her own contempt for vulgar ambitions and self-interest a child only too apt to catch the infection. What he came to call her *espagnolism* —'C'est beau comme le Cid' was her phrase for an action she admired—marked him indelibly. If there were ever the slightest likelihood that he would grow up to be a hard-headed prosperous Beyle, his Gagnon great-aunt nipped it in the bud.

A younger Gagnon, the doctor's son, Romain, amused and excited the quickest senses a child was ever born with. He enormously admired this uncle who was seductively attractive, a dandy, and had mistresses. Could there be a more delicious life? That this friendly laughing young man was a serious and already respected lawyer did not enter his mind. The visit he was allowed to pay to Romain Gagnon and his charming young wife in their country house, when he was eight, ravished him with joy: here, feeling himself liked, he became the gay good child he had been when his mother was alive. Séraphie, his unamiable father, the cold gloomy house in the rue des Vieux-Jésuites, M. Joubert, the uncouth old tutor engaged to give him the rudiments of Latin, were a forgotten nightmare: it closed round him again when he went back to Grenoble, to an existence in which his only friends were two family servants who loved him and tried to protect him from Séraphie, and the two old people he clung to as his natural parents. He had no friends of his own age; one of his sharpest griefs during these years was that his father and Séraphie refused to let him meet or speak to other children.

In March next year harmless old Joubert, with his little Latin and torn dirty frock coat, died, and after an interval of a few months, Henri, not yet ten, was handed over body and soul to a much younger and more authoritative tutor. The loathing he conceived for this man remained in him, a living nerve, to the end of his life. Thin, short, ugly, with evasive eyes and a detestable smile, Abbé

Raillane was a cold bigot, unfeeling and autocratic, and his effect on an irrepressibly rebellious child was wholly bad. Save that he was very clean, very *soigné*, he conformed exactly to his volatile pupil's image of a priest, drawn from his memory of the pock-marked abbé he had overheard, the day after his mother died, say that God had done it. From that moment he lumped together God, Séraphie and his father as monsters. It says everything for his innate sweetness that Raillane did not manage to make a counter-bigot of him. All his life the ceremony of the Mass could still move him, and he recalled with smiling pleasure that as a young child he had served with a very decent, very serious air the recalcitrant priests who during the Terror said Mass in his grandfather's drawing-room. He disliked these men intensely. For two other priests he felt something like love, and one, the gay friendly Abbé Chélan who dined with the Gagnons when he came to Grenoble from his country parish, became the model in the *Chartreuse de Parme* for Fabrice's beloved tutor, the astronomer-priest Blanés, and gave his name to the gentle upright curé of Verrières in *Le Rouge et le Noir*. The other, Père Ducros, a singular character, a student of chemistry and botany who had been allowed by the Pope to leave his cloister and become a lay priest, was the city librarian. He lent the eager child books and taught him, to his exquisite pleasure, to mould medals in plaster. Amusements of a solitary child.

For Raillane he felt impotent hatred. He had no defence against a grinding severity except sullenness and lies. They shared a damp, sunless bedroom in the rue des Vieux Jésuites, and the only touch of humanity he recalled in the tutor was the cage of some thirty sickly canaries he placed next to his pupil's bed.

When Louis XVI was condemned as an enemy of the Republic, be sure that the image of another head glimmered in his mind. Why not Raillane, why not Séraphie? Were they, too, not enemies of the Republic? His father's name appeared on the list of suspects drawn up by a fellow-lawyer: with a child's heartless logic he said, 'Amar t'a placé sur la liste comme notoirement *suspect* de ne pas aimer la République, il me semble qu'il est *certain* que tu ne l'aime pas.' During these years Chérubin Beyle was imprisoned three times.

His bloodthirsty young son was not sorry. He rejoiced when two recalcitrant priests were guillotined in the place Grenette, the only killings in Grenoble during the Terror. His outraged aunt was not softened towards him by his anguished grief over another death, that of a young man he loved, his grandfather's manservant, Lambert. It wrenched him as nothing had done since the death of his mother.

Later he made a pitiably absurd attempt to get away from home. A battalion of children from eight to eighteen had been formed in Grenoble under the direction of an unfrocked priest named Gardon. In a faked hand he wrote to his grandfather ordering him to send his grandson to join it and signed the letter: *Salut et fraternité, Gardon*. After their first dismay the family were not taken in, and not amused.

He remained in his tutor's inflexible hands for some twenty months. To a child, an eternity. Then, in August 1794, threatened with arrest as a non-juring priest, Raillane went into hiding in the mountains, and Henri was free.

A month earlier Chérubin Beyle had been finally cleared of suspicion, and released from his third term in prison. He began to spend more and more time on the estate he had inherited from his mother, at Furonières, a village some five miles south-west of Grenoble, in the parish of Claix. He was developing an obsession for it and for agriculture; he had vast plans for making a fortune out of the place and in the meantime spent thought, time, money on it with the seriousness of a gambler possessed of an infallible system. When he could he took his son there with him, walking the distance, and talked to him endlessly about his projects: the boy found them intolerably boring.

There were compensations. Although the area was dry and stony, the estate, on the slope of the mountain, had trees: walnuts, elms, and a splendid avenue of limes. And there were books in the house, on which he seized. They included forty handsomely-bound volumes of Voltaire: he insisted later that even then he had disliked Voltaire, finding him puerile and dry, and since as a child he read in part for the sensuous pleasure he drew from his reading—

as later he listened to music and looked at paintings—it may be true. He had been reading avidly since very early childhood: he seems to have made his most exciting discovery in the Furonières house before the Raillane years. This was an edition in French of *Don Quichotte*, with illustrations that amused him madly. Vexed by his wild laughter his father threatened to take the book from him, and he hid himself with it in the alley of hornbeams at the farthest edge of the grounds.

Allowed to use his grandfather's library, he read everything that came under his hand, everything he was allowed to read and much that he was not; these last included Rousseau, the *Nouvelle Héloïse*, and the abbé Prévost's *Mémoires et aventures d'un homme de qualité*; and a pornographic novel, *Félicia ou mes fredaines*, left behind with others of its kind by his gaillard uncle Romain when he married and went to live in the country. Snatched from the shelf when his grandfather's attention was distracted, it plunged him into 'a torrent of sensual pleasure'. One forgets how acute this one of the pleasures of reading can be in an imaginative and literate child of nine or ten, and how instinctively it is hidden.

Writing forty or so years later in *Vie de Henry Brulard*, he said: 'Dès ce moment ma vocation fut decidée: vivre à Paris en faisant des comédies comme Molière.' True enough— whether or not the thought ever, in this form, crossed a child's mind.

He did not at this time care for Molière's plays. He had found a volume with engravings in the Furonières bookcase: he did not understand very much of it, and the bourgeois characters and incidents disgusted him: they were all too like his father's dreary obsession and the continual talk at home about money. The book which, at this time and in one sense for life, marked him deeply was the *Nouvelle Héloïse*: it was less the sensual delight he got out of it than the image it pressed into him of a supreme love, a passion of body, mind, nerves, spirit: this image pursued him always, however easily he made do with coarser pleasures.

Thanks to his father's increasingly long absences from Grenoble he began to be a little freer. During these times he locked himself in the drawing-room in the rue des Vieux-Jésuites, unused since his mother died, read what he liked, and began, with borrowed feathers, to put together a comedy. Now, for the first time in his life, he went alone into the street. Not yet venturing to go inside it, he sauntered past the reading-room of Falcon's bookshop: he passionately admired Falcon, a man who was too honest a revolutionary to make any money, and appears in *Le Rouge et le Noir* as the bookseller Falcoz in Verrières, and in *Lucien Leuwen* as the proprietor of the reading-room in Nancy where Lieutenant Leuwen had the imprudence to read the wrong journals.

One dark cold evening that winter—it must have been shortly after his twelfth birthday—he took the risk of slipping out to a meeting of the Society of Jacobins, the largest of the revolutionary societies in Grenoble. It was a sharp disappointment. The speeches had none of the seriousness and zeal he had expected, and the place, an ill-lit church, was packed with shabby unwashed sour-smelling men and women. It was his first contact with *the people*. The disillusion, the physical distaste he felt, remained with him. Remained, too, his passion for social justice: he was on their side against their oppressors—so long as he was not asked to live with them.

He suffered the same disillusion when, ignoring Séraphie's anger, he tried to approach the children he had watched enviously at their games in the public garden, and found that they were unpleasantly rough and mannerless.

Writing more than forty years later, 'They poisoned my childhood,' he said of his father and Raillane. They had taught him to protect himself by continual lies and deceit and injected into his veins the sickness of impotent hatred. Is he exaggerating? To a degree, yes. But very certainly it had an effect: his sense of oppression and isolation during the four or five years after his mother died, the years between seven and twelve. A confident, loving and impulsive child learned distrust, of others and of himself. What was a Beyle instinct to hide the spontaneous movements of his mind and heart became an ingrown habit. Bad enough, but it would have been worse for him if he had learned to lie out of pity, out of the fear of hurting.

Two things saved him. The first he took for granted, the warmth, the fastidious pleasures, the approving love of his Gagnon grandfather and great-aunt. The second: his inborn gaiety of spirit, a divine gift.

Chapter 2

HIS NEW FREEDOMS were safe from the tutor who had succeeded Raillane. M. Durand was an amiable fuddy-duddy of fifty, with pretensions to teach Latin and the humanities: he amused his pupil with Ovid's *Metamorphoses* and taught him to put together Latin verse: the lessons took place twice a day, an hour in the morning and another in the afternoon, in his grandfather's house, where, moreover, he now slept, delivered from the melancholy bedroom he had shared with Raillane and the evil-smelling canaries.

His first real break-out came near the end of his thirteenth year, in November 1796, when he was enrolled among the earliest pupils in the newly-formed Central School of Grenoble. His grandfather was one of three members of the committee charged with the choice of professors for a school designed, like the others now being established in every department in the country, to provide a thorough training in mathematics, logic, the natural sciences, general grammar, history, literature and—far from last— the strictest republican sentiments. No doubt it cost his clerical and anti-republican father and Séraphie a sharp pang to see him handed over to the enemy, but they could not at this time have pushed imprudence to the point of refusing to send him. Nor, perhaps, did Chérubin Beyle realise how irrevocably his son was being, not led —he was already committed—but hardened in his determination to learn only what he wanted to learn, to live as he wanted to live, and to get away from Grenoble and the Beyle way of life.

To get away: the deepest impulse, nervous and moral, of his being. During the next three years he had his successes as a pupil, notably in mathematics, and in the course in art conducted by a passionately republican master. Logic and grammar were well taught by one Dupuy de Bordes, of whom he thought little, but it was Dupuy who told him: 'Mon enfant, étudie la Logique de

Condillac, c'est la base de tout.' He did as he was told and, with immense excitement, one of those moments of awakening only the young know, discovered a philosophy, a mental discipline which though he grew out of Condillac animated him through a restless life.

Less than two months after he began to move out of reach of her authority his hated aunt died, after an illness he had barely noticed: she was thirty-six. In a rush of joy he dropped to his knees on the floor of the kitchen and thanked God for a great mercy. He was inclined, when he recalled the incident, to admire his heartlessness: it was one of the few illusions he cherished about himself.

Séraphie gone, and his father increasingly absorbed in the agricultural experiments that were to ruin him, he could amuse himself as he liked. For the first time he was living among boys of his own age. It was not the instant pleasure he had expected: the ruder among them were offended by the fastidiousness and unconscious arrogance of a child brought up as carefully as a marriageable girl and, probably without knowing it, he began to draw the faint outlines of his public face, the reckless talker, the aggressive ironist. Towards the end of his first year it even came to a duel, with pistols, between himself and an older rougher boy; the latter was to fire first, but—their witnesses must have kept their heads—the pistols had not been charged, and the affair ended in an unfriendly truce. If he is to be believed—and why not?—in the moment of waiting to be shot at he discovered that he could control panic by an act of imaginative energy, concentrating his mind on an immediate detail, in this instance the contour of a small rock behind his opponent's head. He was a little young to make this discovery, but genius is demonstrably not a matter of age, and he had already learned, too early, a horror of being seen to care what was happening to him.

Not long after this he fell wildly in love with a young actress—for the first time since his uncle took him, aged six, to a performance of Le Cid, he had begun going to the theatre. Virginie Kubly was barely eighteen and he not yet fifteen; it was the mould for all his adult passions, the feverish obsession, the diffidence, the clumsiness;

he never spoke to her, and at a chance glimpse of her in the street almost lost consciousness. Oddly, her thin little voice singing a wretched air by Gaveaux woke in him a feeling for music, half rational, half sensuous, that outlasted in him every other intellectual passion except that for Shakespeare. When her engagement at the theatre ended and she left Grenoble, he was emotionally and morally ravaged—perhaps not for so long as he expected.

The Henri Beyle who adored good company and talk was beginning to emerge; he made a few close friends he never lost, though his judgement of them changed somewhat with time: there was Louis de Barral, well-bred and easy in hand; Félix Faure, the most mature of the group of lively adolescents, the most clearly marked for worldly success; Romain Colomb, his cousin, whose father like his own had been a political prisoner; and that Louis Crozet whose morose image, stiffening as he aged, stretched like a line of milestones across Henri's life: he was short on humour, touchy, irritably insistent on his superior acuteness, intellect, sagacity—and possessed of all three—and unattractive even as a boy, clumsy, graceless, heavily pock-marked face, red-rimmed eyes, and with it all devoted to Beyle, his most painstaking critic, advising, labouring over his manuscripts. If, at times, Beyle found him indigestible, he never ceased to value him: he knew what he had in this one of his friends.

Early in his second year at the school he made the friend with whom, for the first time in his life, almost for the last, he had the intoxicating experience of being able to talk his head off in the certainty that he was accepted and liked without reserve. The three young Bigillions were living alone, except for a young servant, in a small third-floor apartment which their parents, country people living outside Grenoble, rented for them during school terms. It was an engagingly innocent community of two brothers and a sister: the eldest, François, sixteen; Victorine, fifteen (Henri's age); and Rémy, fourteen. He spent hours with François, walking, talking endlessly, the unafraid outpouring of ideas and beliefs only possible at the age they were. François was singularly without any need to pretend that he knew all about the world and women, and passionately certain that friendship is from the gods themselves. The younger brother, Rémy, jealously wounded by the intimacy between the other two, watched uneasily the growing warmth between his sister and Beyle: in fact it was as innocent as everything in the life lived in the little apartment, the gaiety, the plain country food sent every week by the parents and carefully shared out by Victorine: Henri talked to her as easily as to her brothers, she was simple and natural, and he admired her young figure, but did not fall in love with her. It was a first flicker of the liking a mature Beyle felt for one or two women, those on whom he relied for a gentleness and understanding of which a child had been robbed. Recalling it, he said: 'Nous vivons alors comme de jeunes lapins jouant dans un bois tout en broutant le serpolet.'

Pity for too bright a spirit. François Bigillion married young, in 1802. There is a letter from him written two years later. 'Tout à mes yeux est confus; je n'ai nulle ordre dans mes idées. . . . Comment puis-je être si malheureux? Ma femme se porte bien, m'aime toujours autant: mon fils est auprès de moi. . . . Toi, Beyle, tu me dis que je suis le seul, ton meilleur ami. Mais es-tu le mien, Henri? L'es-tu mon ami comme je suis le tien?' Stendhal drew him to the life in *Le Rouge et le Noir*, in that François Fouqué completely and sensitively devoted to Julien Sorel. That was in 1830, three years after François Bigillion killed himself. The later reference to him in the *Vie de Henry Brulard* has a dry sound: 'Vers ce temps-là je me liai, je ne sais comment, avec François Bigillion (qui depuis s'est tué, je crois, par ennui de sa femme.)' The moving portrait of Fouqué remains.

Beyle's second year at school ended in a triumph, with the first prize for literature and a second in mathematics. He was very pleased with himself—and no less pleased and excited a week later when he shot at and killed his first thrush, at Furonières; he remembered and recorded every detail of the incident, and of the second and third victims, and although he says that, later, when he was administrating the occupied province of Brunswick, he became disgusted with the habit of killing animals for sport, his revulsion does not seem to have gone so far as to save small birds from his marksmanship: at Civitavecchia, two years before he died, he was still killing larks and quails.

In November, at the start of his third year, his life changed direction or rather emphasis. He had been well tutored in the classics, Corneille, Molière, Saint-Simon, Racine (the last, for all his later brisk sallies against 'cet adroit courtisan nommé Racine' marked him: think of two of his greatest figures, Sorel and Count Mosca, both of them, in their way, out of Racine), by a professor who went so far as to give his pupils a little Shakespeare. It was enough to start in young Beyle a lasting passion. From an uncle, François Bigillion borrowed for him the volumes of Letourneur's translation, passing them to him one by one. Not at once, but soon, within five or six years, his admiration became a compelling love, so much part of him that he could not have torn it away. At the moment he was in the grip of another idea—call it an obsession. Not yet sixteen, he had learned not only to avoid as far as he could the risk of being laughed at for his ambitions, but to choose between them. At that age very difficult. He was exceptionally singleminded about himself. He took no advice, even of the grandfather he had clung to: consciously or not, he was outgrowing Dr Gagnon. His decision was an emotional one, but he took it coolly. A mastery of higher mathematics was the surest chance he had of mastering life itself and, before all, of escaping from a suffocatingly bigoted provincial society. He would have been put to it later to say at what point in his childhood he had realised that he must escape from Grenoble, 'cette fange qui me fait mal au cœur'. It was impossible for him to make a name for himself here. With mathematics he could get to Paris and the École Polytechnique. Very sensible—but not the whole of what he was thinking, and not, finally, the deciding factor. The other side of this resolve was a blindness to every consideration except the one uppermost in his mind at the moment. Blindness which—not that he ever realised it—was responsible for most of the errors of his life and for its triumphant success. 'En vérité ai-je dirigé le moins du monde ma vie?' he asked himself later. He had, but without a glance at the price.

His hatred of Grenoble was venomous: 'Tout ce qui est bas et plat dans le genre bourgeois me rappelle Grenoble,' he wrote in *Brulard*, 'tout ce qui me rappelle Grenoble me fait horreur, non, *horreur* est trop noble, *mal au cœur*. Grenoble est pour moi comme le souvenir d'une abominable indigestion, il n'y a pas de danger mais un effroyable dégoût. Tout ce qui est bas et plat sans compensation, tout ce qui est ennemi du moindre mouvement généreux, tout ce qui se réjouit du malheur de qui aime la patrie ou est généreux, voilà Grenoble pour moi.'

He confounded his father with his detestation of the city; all he wanted, he said, was to get away from a person for whom he felt neither tolerance nor liking. All no doubt a genuine emotion, but the point to remember is that abhorrence of Grenoble was the form taken by a passion.

From now on he slaved at mathematics. He made a perplexed nuisance of himself to his tutors by questioning axioms he was required to take as evident: they were anything but evident to him and he concluded that Professor Dupuy de Bordes was cheating, and fretted until he had got himself to a coach, a young man, Gabriel Gros, who was both a good mathematician and an ardent revolutionary and taught an adoring pupil very soundly.

In a sense, the most he got out of his competence, so far as it went, in mathematics, was a confirmation and heightening of the virtues of lucidity and concision learned as a child in the Gagnon drawing-room. He never advanced very far into higher mathematics, he had started too late: in any event, for him it was the means to an end, not the passion itself. He enjoyed it, sharpened his teeth on it, and it served its purpose. In September 1799 he scored a second and weightier triumph: the first prize in mathematics and a citation. The road to Paris and the École Polytechnique was open, and his only anxiety now was whether his father would allow a sixteen-year-old to go to Paris, that sink of iniquity, and give him the money to live there.

Somehow it was arranged. A few weeks later, when he left Grenoble, his father cried, a sight his unforgiving son found extremely ugly. This is something sharper than the embarrassment an adolescent feels when a parent weeps over him. He was incapable of sympathy or pity for this sealed soul, which is not only natural, all things considered, but on the whole a good thing; the child brought up to pity a father or mother for any but the most serious of reasons is emotionally warped. Chérubin Beyle's tears sprang out of the realisation that his son felt for him only dislike and a mad joy in getting away. We hear of him crying again, five or six years later, when he is showing Dr Gagnon a bitter letter from Henri in Paris. He had handled his son badly from the start, but would he ever have been able to do better than bore him? They were born to disagree, he was rebarbative and rigid, and such sensibility and tenderness as he had were not attractive.

Chapter 3

HE ARRIVED IN Paris on 10 November 1799, having heard the evening before, in Nemours, and rejoiced over it, of the *coup d'état* that made Napoleon master of France.

He had with him the certificate, the *brevet de civisme*, which opened the École Polytechnique to scholars of impeccable republican principles, but he had no intention of using it. All along his plan, growing in him from the early years when he began to be a passionate reader, reading in his grandfather's library, had been to live in Paris, have mistresses, and write comedies like Molière. So he insists, and there is no reason to doubt it. A solitary child, in revolt against everything he understood of his father's values and ambitions, with the liveliest of minds, what was he likely to dream about if not about a life as erotically exciting as he imagined his attractive young uncle to live and as cultivated as his admired grandfather's? He had intoxicated himself with the thought of becoming the new Molière as obsessively as with sexual dreams of seducing a Kubly. There was not enough, though there was some, of the Dauphinois shrewdness, patience, cunning, hard common-sense in him, to rouse the need to begin by making himself safe. Turning his back on the École was the overt sign of the reckless streak in him, the first act of deliberate imprudence—deliberate, planned, reasoned imprudence, and fatal because reasoned.

His allowance from his father was one hundred and fifty francs a month, enough, under the Consulate and the Empire, for him to live moderately well, but he had no sense of economy, and disdained the advice of fellow-students from Grenoble to watch his pocket. After a few days in a *hôtel meublé* used by students of the École, he settled himself in a house where several of his Grenoble school friends were living. Then he moved to a cheap furnished room looking on to the rue du Bac. Paris disappointed him. He

29

found it ugly; it was dirty and there were no mountains. Sadly, too, no charming young actress offered herself to his inexperience: and he was too fastidious as well as too timid to make do with one of the easy women with whom his friends amused themselves. At the end of the year, between boredom and bad food he fell ill in his cold, seedy lodging, and into the hands of a quack used to doctoring the gonorrhoeas of the École, whose medicines were no use to him. He became really ill. He was rescued from his misery by the one influential acquaintance he had in Paris. M. Daru was Dr Gagnon's first cousin, a handsome old gentleman in his late sixties, comfortably off and prepared to do his duty by a member of the family; he summoned a nurse and a famous doctor, and as soon as it could be done moved his young relative to his own house. Here he was given a room on an inner courtyard looking across gardens. He was pleased with it, but not happy.

He was profoundly dissatisfied with himself. Nothing in his provincial upbringing had prepared him to face polite Parisian society, and the Daru salon intimidated him horribly. Dinner was a torture; he was awkward and mortifyingly tongue-tied, he did not dare open his mouth and dreaded the moment when he had to give his arm to one of M. Daru's daughters, Mlle Sophie or Madame Cambon or Madame de Brun, or to Madame Daru herself, gentle and withdrawn. After thirty-six years the memory of his discomfort was still alive: ' . . . moi qui, me croyant une disposition infinie à aimer et être aimé, croyais que l'occasion seule me manquait, je me trouvais inférieur et gauche en tout dans une société que je jugeais triste et maussade. . . . C'était donc là ce Paris que j'avais tant désiré!' (*Brulard*)

A social failure, disliking Paris, even to the cooking. His disillusion was complete. But—this is important—the experience strengthened in him, perhaps without his knowing it, the seeds of a liking for solitude no less deep in him than his delight in intelligent company, an isolation in which he was safe from a half-conscious dread of failure, social failure, sexual failure, failure to become a great writer. He did not surrender to it for an instant: timidity was matched and overmatched in him by an unabateable confidence.

He was happier with the Rebuffels, mother and daughter, living on the same side of the courtyard, immediately below his room. Madame Rebuffel's husband was a nephew of M. Daru and a pleasant fellow who, when he was in Paris, lived with his mistress but spent a quarter of an hour every day with his wife. In this gayer less formal household, Henri Beyle recovered his tongue and his vivacity: he took lessons from a dancer at the Opéra and danced with the eleven-year-old Adèle Rebuffel, a young charmer. He was at his ease, too, with the younger of M. Daru's two sons, the twenty-five-year-old Martial Daru, a second Romain Gagnon, good-tempered, lively, fortunate with women, ready to be carelessly kind to a half-fledged young provincial.

His first letter to his sister Pauline was written this year, in March, perhaps at some moment when his loneliness and disappointment were biting him. He could have written sooner. In their childhood she had been his devoted disciple, enthusiastically adopting all his loves and aversions, even to his hatred of their father. She was fourteen now, leading a dull life among elderly people. This first letter strikes the note of the long series of marvellous and on occasion absurdly ingenuous letters he sent her during the next decade. They were such as he might have written to a young brother he loved very much and wanted anxiously to form, and he invested her, a pleasant very ordinary young girl, with all the qualities he admired, wit, intelligence, eagerness to learn. The list of writers she must not fail to read included Plutarch, Rousseau, Racine, Voltaire, and this is only a beginning: he overwhelmed her with vast schemes of self-education and self-examination, sometimes naïve but never merely clever. His zeal was largely misdirected, but what moved him was love, a warm lively impulse to keep her beside him. In a sense he was writing to himself, to the reflection of himself, an exception wanting to be like and yet to surpass others, to be admired, accepted, safe.

He had come to Paris with a serious purpose: in his pleasant room he read through the four volumes of Cailhava's *L'Art de la Comédie*, bought when he arrived, and began to write a play. His verses did not please him. Perhaps he would be wiser to attempt an opera: Grétry might be simpler to outdo than Molière. Or to take up painting. Recognising that he knew little of either art, he registered himself at the École des Beaux Arts. He did not have time to get very far. Shocked to his stiff prudent backbone that his *cher cousin* had simply neglected to sit for the entrance to the École Polytechnique, M. Daru gave him a severe talking-to, all the more crushing for its icy politeness, and a few days later told him that he had arranged with his elder son, just returned from a visit to the army, to take him into his department in the War Office. He obeyed, of course. Still half schoolboy, within a few days of his seventeenth birthday, what else could he do? And perhaps, though he never says so, he was not altogether sorry to be given the chance to find his way in a perplexing world where, so far, freedom had not brought him the satisfactions he expected.

Pierre Daru at this time was chief of the First Bureau in the War Office and, at thirty-two, marked for exceptional success. Highly intelligent, highly cultivated, a man of probity, courage, moral energy, he was also brutally authoritative and ill-tempered. He drove himself as hard as he drove his subordinates. An atmosphere of terror hung over his department. Thanks to his obscurity, Henri Beyle escaped with little worse than savage sarcasms directed at his uncertain spelling and appalling handwriting: even apart from the differences in age, breeding, protocol, there was no possibility of warmth between two such dissimilar characters. The continual blunders and what he saw as the innate levity and incompetence of his young relative made an ineffaceable impression on Pierre Daru: years later, when he caught sight in a bookshop of a rare copy of the first edition of Stendhal's *Rome, Naples et Florence* and asked the price, he burst into a roar of laughter, 'Impossible! That child, ignorant as a carp!' The fact remains—a fact Henri Beyle himself recognised later, as he recognised and did justice to the elder man's uprightness—that so long as Henri Beyle was dependent on him, Daru protected and did what he could for a young man who, unmanageable as he proved himself, was *of the family*.

It rested with young Beyle himself to climb, or not to climb.

The ladder was there. But I doubt that even in his coolest moments he reflected that he was faced with a choice. He did his work—badly. He was bored by it—as all his life he was bored by routine—and bored by his fellow-clerks, in spite of lively arguments with the head clerk on the relative merits of Racine and Shakespeare. He could not at this time even write a passable official letter. The other life, the life of reading, and writing masterpieces, which when he set out from Grenoble he had seen as his future, had dropped out of sight. Outside the office he was nagged by a confused impatience; he had got himself into a blind alley and he had no coherent idea how to escape.

He had an object lesson under his eyes in young Edmond Cardon, who was his age, charming, high-spirited, keen, with an ambitious well-connected mother determined to advance him. The friendship between the Darus and Cardons was close, and Beyle was neither surprised nor, he insists, envious, except of the delightful uniform that went with the appointment, when in April Pierre Daru had Edmond made *adjoint aux commissaires des guerres*. Writing in 1836, he saw clearly enough what he had done, or rather had failed to do at the beginning of his career. He had had chances to make himself safe, rich, respected, and had either not noticed or omitted to use them. Wit, originality, are not enough. He blamed, probably with tongue in cheek, the elder Daru for not telling him plainly that success depends on finesse and tact, on making the right friends, becoming intimate with influential people, being seen in the right houses. In sober truth, it would have been no use if he had been warned in 1800, or at any time. What he was then he remained. To say that there were no moments when he was mortified by his lack of worldly respect and success would not be true, but in fact he had no more choice than a man born blind has between seeing and not seeing. And he knew it.

Freedom from routine came after little more than five months in Paris, when Pierre Daru arranged for him to follow himself and Martial, and Napoleon's victorious army, to Italy. Wild with joy, he left on the 7th of May in civilian dress, with pistols and an enormous portmanteau weighted with books. He had orders to pick up in Geneva a convalescent horse Daru had left there. Two weeks later, having armed himself further with spurs and a long heavy sabre, he loaded the horse with himself and the portmanteau and started out from Geneva: it was only the second or third time he had been on horseback; the young beast was fresh and bolted with him. He had the luck to be taken in hand by a somewhat disreputable Captain Burelvillers, perhaps a mere *chevalier d'industrie*, who, appalled by his ignorance and ineptness, gave him lessons in riding and the handling of a sabre, cheated him, mildly enough, in the matter of their expenses in inns, and probably saved him from worse hazards along a route crowded with Napoleon's troops: he had not thought to take a servant and he had money on him.

He had never been as happy. The view across Lake Léman after he left Geneva was a breaking delight; as close as he ever came to pure happiness, a few minutes worth in themselves the trouble of living: 'J'ai recherché avec une sensibilité exquise la vue des beaux paysages,' he wrote in *Brulard*; 'c'est pour cela uniquement que j'ai voyagé. Les paysages étaient comme un archet qui jouait sur mon âme.'

On 28 May they crossed the St Bernard Pass; I am in Italy, he told himself, in Italy. The descent on the other side, steep rocky paths, precipices, melting snow, mist, had dangers for an inexperienced rider that he was young and ignorant enough to take lightly. Making their way through the lower hills towards Ivrea, they were caught in the confusion round the old heavily fortified Fort Bard in which a small body of Austrians was still holding out against the French troops, and had to work their way by difficult mule tracks across the side of Mont Albarado after a night when they bivouacked off the road and Beyle's delicate skin was martyred by mosquitoes, an inglorious detail he left out when he was making the most of the incident in a letter of 29th of June to Pauline from Milan: 'Nous avons grimpé la montagne sous le feu continuel du fort. Ce qui nous a fait le plus de peine ç'a été nos chevaux qui à chaque sifflement de boulet ou d'obus se precipitaient de cinq ou six pieds.'

What happened to him in Ivrea—or it may have been in Novaro, a night or two farther on—was as religious an event as any conversion; the very phrases he used thirty-six years later to describe it are unconsciously those of the mystics. Against the advice of Burelvillers, cynically sure that his sabre would get him into trouble in a town full of soldiers, he took himself to the opera, where a fifth-rate company was singing Cimarosa's *Matrimonio Segreto*. The only detail he remembered about the spectacle was that the actress who sang Caroline had lost a front tooth, but the music ravished him; he was possessed suddenly by a rending pleasure; henceforth all he wanted was to live in Italy and hear Italian music. Certainly it was not all he wanted, not even all an absurdly exalted young man on a May evening in 1800 wanted, but the experience was decisive: without the revelation of Cimarosa, at this moment, in this place, would Milan, would Italy have seduced him as it did? And without the years in Italy would he, through all changes, all errors, have gone on to write the *Chartreuse de Parme*?

He and his companion left Ivrea on the 2nd of June. Every moment of the road to Milan was a lively pleasure. The countryside of Lombardy, trees, mountains, even the fields of maize, enraptured him. The journey was not without its hazards from groups of skirmishing Austrians, and they travelled slowly, in convoy; it was probably not much before the 10th or 11th that he entered Milan on a delicious spring morning, 'et quel printemps! et dans quel pays du monde!'

The first person he saw—he recalled the street and the precise point in it—was Martial Daru, who took him straight to their quarters in the superb Casa d'Adda; its splendour overwhelmed him, as did Milan itself: the five or six months he spent there were possibly the happiest of his whole life, 'un intervalle de bonheur fou et complet'. For a time he worked in Pierre Daru's bureau, under the *commissaire des guerres* Louis Joinville, with whose mistress he fell wildly in love. Angela Pietragrua, a black-haired opulent twenty-three, married to a clerk in the Weights and Measures department, was what he later called her, 'a whore, but

35

a sublime whore'. She was a superb young animal. Too timid to try for her favours, he delivered himself over to her imagined being: she obsessed him, and the obsession persisted, much as the odour of a rank spice persists, until eleven years later he succeeded with her, briefly.

He says very casually in *Brulard* that during this first visit to Milan he lost his innocence, but he could not remember with whom: what he does not say is that he was infected, and treated with mercury: his biographers and annotators have spent time trying to decide whether it was for syphilis or gonorrhoea and, more serious, whether the feverish ills that plagued him several times afterwards and his death from apoplexy forty years later are partly to be blamed on this adolescent misfortune.

Pierre Daru had handed him over, after six weeks, to his own powerful friend and patron, Claude Petiet, at that time Minister Extraordinary to the French government in northern Italy. He worked in Petiet's bureau, had a room in the ambassadorial palace, a taste of social grandeur, so far as a seventeen-year-old subordinate can enjoy it, and became friendly with Petiet's two elder sons Alexandre and Augustine, respectively eighteen and sixteen, in the first stage of their successful careers. With Alexandre he fought a duel, with sabres, over a pretty woman who cared nothing for him or his youthful opponent, and was wounded in the left foot.

He was still socially diffident, dreading the moment when he had to tip a footman. None the less, during these months he was continually and acutely happy. It was the light of Italy, it was his freedom, it was the gaiety of Milan, the balls, the music, the evenings at the Scala, the cafés, the loveliness of the countryside; it was the fever of first youth.

Did Pierre Daru already suspect that what Dr Gagnon's grandson dreamed of was a life in which he read, learned, heard music, and talked and laughed with friends? Probably not. He can hardly have imagined that even given his crass incompetence as a clerk, the young man could be quite so lightminded. So, willing to do his best for him, he prepared to advance him in the administrative side of the army, his own side. The trouble was that entry into QMG (Corps de l'Intendance) demanded three years' service as an officer and passing an examination in mathematics and army administration. Pierre Daru's lines of influence were equal to the strain: in September Henri Beyle was commissioned in the cavalry as temporary second-lieutenant, and a month later, on the initiative of Général Davout himself, the 'proche parent de l'inspector Daru' was attached to the Sixth Dragoons. Wearing the splendid uniform, green with scarlet revers, white cloak, gilded helmet with the long black horsetail, he joined his corps at the village of Bagnolo near Brescia. The Commandant of the Sixth, Colonel le Baron, a friend of Daru's, obliged with the necessary certificate of active service with the regiment.

Bagnolo was a squalid hole. Writing to Pauline on the 7th of December he complained of the savagery of the natives, 'des brutes à figure humaine qui habitent ce pays'. He was not forced to endure its discomforts very long. Here the ground begins to shake a little under our feet. He had been warmly recommended to Général Michaud by his former chief in Pierre Daru's bureau in Milan, Joinville, and later in the month he was in Milan: from there between the 23rd and the 31st of December he wrote letters to Pauline. In after years he talked about the fighting on the Mincio river, where the Sixth Dragoons were engaged on Christmas Day, and the taking of Castelfranco on the 12th of January when Général Michaud directed the attack. He cannot have been at the Mincio crossing, but he could have been at Castelfranco: a certificate he asked for and got from Michaud four years later says that he distinguished himself there by his bravery. True, he wrote it himself, but Michaud's signature is that of a soldier with a serious reputation not only for courage but for honesty and integrity. He missed the Mincio engagement, but I see no reason to reject his account, no doubt sharpened, of Castelfranco.

Back to solid ground. In February he became a personal ADC to Michaud: he was then in Milan on some errand for him, rejoined him in Mantua, was with him at Verona and at Milan again in April. Years hence he recalled an evening in the Scala when he met the author of *Liaisons Dangereuses*, now an old man. Hearing that

37

the young officer came from Grenoble, Général Choderlos de Laclos was deeply moved. In the journal he began to keep at this time Beyle does not mention the incident. Was it one that only *ought* to have happened?

His agreeably varied existence on the staff was suddenly threatened. A War Ministry order had laid down that only full lieutenants with two campaigns to their credit were eligible to serve as aides-de-camp, and early in May a letter from the Commandant of the Sixth Dragoons instructed him to return to his regiment at Savigliano. Engrossed, apart from the hardly onerous duties of his office, in translating a play of Goldoni's and taking lessons in playing the clarinet, he put it out of his mind. Infuriated warnings from Pierre Daru that he was wasting time and losing chances had no effect on him: the ladder his powerful relative had set up for him was an irrelevance; he had other ambitions. He succeeded in staying where he was, in Bergamo and then in Brescia, for another four months, when higher authority lost patience and ordered his general to return him. On the 30th of September, by way of a very pleasant week in Milan, he reached Bra and his squadron. Here he was bored, bored, bored. Bored by garrison life, bored by manoeuvres, bored above all by his brother-officers and their low level of conversation and intelligence. In October he fell feverishly ill. True, he was capable of falling ill only from boredom and restlessness, but it was perhaps a flare-up of the infection in Milan? He put in for sick leave. It was granted from the end of the year.

Did he, when he left to go to Grenoble, intend never to return as a soldier? In fact it was ten years before he saw Italy again. During all that time it smouldered in his nerves and mind. He was no longer the ingenuous adolescent, madly happy to be in Italy and in love, but he was not a whit closer to the Daru model of a politic young man with sensible well-judged aims and intentions. Restless, desperately conscious of time slipping past without his having taken a firm step towards any of the fledgling ambitions beating in his mind, he knew more clearly what he did not want than how to seize and shape what he did.

Chapter 4

BACK IN GRENOBLE he was not sorry to find that Chérubin Beyle disliked so sourly having his son in the Republican army that he was willing to make him a yearly allowance of, well, it might be three thousand francs, if he resigned. This suited him very well: he asked nothing better than to go back to Paris and live *en philosophe*—his phrase—no doubt with a side glance towards amusements he was more habited to now than when he rode into Milan. In the meantime he had conjured himself into love with a girl of his own age. Victorine Mounier was the daughter of an astute and intelligent political lawyer who had owed the start of his career—he was the son of a Grenoble draper—to Dr Gagnon's help. Not the least astute of his moves had been to emigrate to Switzerland in 1790: he had spent the last five years in Weimar and was in Paris now, attaching himself to the First Consul. His daughter's stay in Grenoble was likely to be brief, and Beyle was not able to make the most of it. When he met her socially he was tongue-tied and diffident: away from her he gave himself up to the delight of evoking the charming details of incidents which never took place. In March her father summoned her to join him in Paris. With a headful of furious strategies, and the works of Cabanis, Montesquieu and Destutt de Tracy, Beyle hurried after her. A month later, without his having spoken to her or set eyes on her, she left Paris, when Joseph Mounier was named Préfet of the department of Ille-et-Vilaine. He stood in pouring rain under a carriage entrance in the rue Montmartre and watched her leave for Rennes. After this he had the youthfully asinine idea of writing to her brother Édouard, not one of his close friends, letters he hoped she would be shown: they were filled with stories of amorous successes and awkward allusions to his longing for a pure love. Though a year younger than Beyle, Édouard Mounier was shrewd and cool-headed, amiable enough, but a proper

Dauphinois: out of kindness or with a flicker of irony he wrote back for a time, in somewhat moralising tones, but did not show his sister the fool's letters.

A self-induced passion can be as violent and absorbing as any other of the kinds of love. This fantasy which Beyle clung to with characteristic persistence for at least three years was only peculiar for its shadowy basis. During these three years he may have seen the young woman three times. He saw her for a moment in 1804 when she came to Paris for the festivities at Napoleon's coronation. He came face to face with her by accident as she was leaving the house. 'J'ai l'honneur de vous saluer, mademoiselle,' was all he was able to say. She made him a brief curtsy and passed on without speaking. Thackeray, smiling gently at the fatuity of his young hero, could not have planned a more ridiculously touching scene. It was the effective end of his obsession, but with his sister he kept up the fable of a hopeless love: years later, when Victorine married, he told Pauline's husband, 'I had some days of violent grief,' and for a year or so longer there are wistful references to her in his letters. When, in *Brulard*, he is listing the names of women who have occupied his life hers is not among them: none the less she is one of the infatuations which set the pattern of his inner life as, in his own words, that of an unlucky lover.

An intellectual love can sit very easily with more fleshly satisfactions. As soon as he arrived in Paris he called on the Rebuffels, the mother and daughter with whom in his first awful weeks in 1799 he had been happier than with the Darus. Adèle, at fourteen an accomplished flirt, was too cool to allow admirers more than a graceful caress. He was very easily seducible when attacked with gaiety and a degree of tenderness, and Madame Rebuffel, still a charming and very pretty woman, allowed herself to seduce him. His Journal fixes 25 August 1802 as the day she took him. So now he enjoyed both a compliant mistress and her daughter's provoking kisses.

It would be a gross error to forget that he had come to Paris with a purpose in which neither Victorine nor any of his tangible pleasures counted a breath. *He* did not forget it.

During the first month he lodged in the same house as his friend Félix Faure, then moved to a room on the sixth floor of the hôtel de Rouen, 153 rue d'Angivillier; it had a view to the colonnade of the Louvre. His real life was lived here. Or was it? The reality of any life, the humblest or the most dedicated, is painfully, mortifyingly fissured. The least one can say is that he passed the greater part of his time in this room, working with intense concentration. He had written to the War Office to resign his commission, rejecting the friendly attempt of Général Michaud to persuade him to stay in the army with a place on his staff. He rejected it as lightheartedly as he had rejected the École Polytechnique, with the same baseless confidence. A note made a year later, in May 1803, runs: 'Quel est mon but? D'être le plus grand poète possible. Pour cela connaître parfaitement l'homme.' The single one of his obsessions he never, from childhood in Grenoble to sudden death in Paris, altered by a heart's impulse.

Providing himself with more books than he, or rather Chérubin Beyle, could easily afford, he read avidly: among the rest Montaigne, Montesquieu, Rousseau—criticising, upbraiding him for his emotional incontinence—La Bruyère, de Retz, Alfieri, Tasso, Corneille, Racine, and always and always Shakespeare. He struggled to read him in English, taking lessons from Father Jéki, an Irish Franciscan. His feelings towards Racine were still ambiguous: he admired, coldly, and found him inferior to Corneille, devoid of tenderness and sincerity, 'courtisan rempli d'adresse et de bien-dire'. He read in libraries, visited museums, followed courses at the Collège de France. He translated from Vergil and Tasso. He seized on and devoured the works of Helvétius, Hobbes, Cabanis, Locke, and as a devoutly respectful disciple Destutt de Tracy, ideologist of the school of Condillac and Locke. To innumerable pages filled with reflections and analyses he added the notes and drafts for a never completed *Filosofia nova*, abandoning it after some three years as a disordered mass of researches, speculations, reveries, the *disjecta membra* of a science of human nature. What is of living interest in it, what fascinates, is the pulse of an unwearying curiosity, strengthening in him like a child in the womb. The nineteen-year-old settling himself in his shabby room in the rue d'Angivillier knew he could not get himself the familiar knowledge he wanted, 'connaissance exacte des hommes', simply by absorbing other men's learning. Or by botanising his friends and acquaintances, as he did. The study of logic and philosophy was important: the study of human nature essential: to examine himself, his motives and impulses, with the impersonality of a surgeon dissecting a body. He had started a journal in Milan; and he kept it during the next twenty or so years. What is more, he kept the promise he made to himself when he began it, to record himself without vanity or pretences, or moralising. Its sincerity is as palpable as a thread of cold air in a closed room; and so is the indefinable distance between us and this *cœur mis à nu*, the measure, perhaps, of the effort he was making to look at himself as if he were looking at another man, or at an animal. The Journal was a vital part of his self-education: without exaggeration it can be said that, here, more than in any of his writings of the period, the creator of Julien Sorel and Count Mosca was creating himself. His first masterpiece.

He must have realised rather quickly that he had neither the time nor the aptitude to write a philosophical treatise. The place for an apprentice poet, the rival of Molière, was the theatre, and his task the turning of everything he learned about human motives, follies, virtues into speaking likenesses of men and women. He spent the greater number of his evenings in the Théâtre-Française, listening, looking, every sense alert. He became friendly with actors and actresses: Martial Daru, with whom he was now on the footing of another young man about town, took him to the Opéra and into the dressing-room of a well-known dancer, who let the two of them remain while she undressed and dressed. Many of his working hours were given up to a close reading of the great dramatists, and writing long commentaries on them. He made a study of rhythms in verse and prose. He began a *Hamlet*, and wisely put it aside 'for six years, by which time I shall be sure of my style'. Ideas for plays swarmed in his head: some got no farther than lists of titles, others may have been destroyed, others exist only as drafts, scattered scenes, fragments of dialogue. A brilliant dramatic critic in the making; a playwright, no. He was incapable of subduing himself, his native subtlety and sensitivity and his passionate interest in his own impulses and motives, to that discipline. He wrestled for more than twenty years before realising that for him comedy and tragedy could breathe and stretch their limbs only in the novel.

He worked on and off for two years on a blank verse play, *Deux Hommes*, struggling desperately with his alexandrines, and dropped it for a satiric comedy called *Letellier*. This he expected to finish quickly; in fact he carried it about with him for more than fifteen years, taking it up at long intervals and enriching it, to suffocation, from his massive notes for characters and situations. In spite of its flashes of wit and insight it died of the method, but not for some twenty-seven years. He worked on it sporadically in Marseille when he was not at his clerking or engaged with his young mistress; and again during two years in Paris as an energetic Auditor to the Conseil d'État: he took it with him to Moscow in 1812, to Milan in 1816, and to Paris and London in 1821. A few twitches of life in 1830—the very year of *Le Rouge et le Noir*: he tried for a moment to interest Mérimée in it. That was the end; the end, too, of a child's spontaneous decision to be the new Molière. I daresay he smiled; he had nothing to regret.

Least of all to regret the twenty years spent teaching himself to write dialogue in which every syllable counts, to allow his characters to give themselves and their unrealised intentions away in action; and above all to avoid over-emphasis and false sentiments. Though it did not serve to make him the greatest dramatist of his time, it gave him his individual mastery of the novel. No other discipline would have so suppled in his style his natural virtues, clarity, wit, spontaneity, lightness of foot, so sharpened the knife he uses against what he called 'mes deux bêtes d'aversion', hypocrisy and vagueness.

He writes in more than one place of his fierce hunger for fame: to write a masterpiece, to be well-known, respected, rich, to be accepted in cultivated intelligent society: the last an adult version of his memories of the Gagnon household. His ambitions raged in him, an obscure young man in a poor room, sure of his genius, sure of future glory. Happy young fool. He should have known that laborious efforts to write with complete sincerity and truth are not a recipe for success, unless, and not always then, as a human being. In fact he sometimes knew it, even then. 'Je pourrais faire une ouvrage qui ne plairait qu'à moi, qui serait reconnu beau en 2000.' (31 December 1804)

The three or four years after his return to Paris in April 1802 were probably the most carefree of his life. His only anxiety was the common juvenile one of lack of money. We need not be sorry for him. Not only was he not without resources; he was young. Writing to his sister on the 10th of June 1804 he told her: '... je portais depuis huit jours des souliers percés, et j'avais besoin de tout mon esprit pour glisser sous le trou une petite patte teinte en noir avec de l'encre. Je dois à la pension où je mange ... je dois à mon portier; je dois à mon tailleur, qui venait me voir tous les matins; il y a longtemps que ma montre est engagée. Je ne vais nulle part depuis quinze jours, faute d'avoir douze sous dans ma poche; je néglige M. Daru, le général Michaud, mademoiselle Duchesnois! que de raisons de me désespérer! Eh bien, jamais je n'ai tant ri. ...'

It is true he was often short of money. Only too pleased to have got him out of the army his father had promised him an allowance larger than he could well afford. Though the sums he sent were fairly adequate, he did not always send them on time; there were disastrous gaps. But Chérubin Beyle was financially straitened himself, and with all his awkward inarticulate affection for his son can only have found the young man's prodigal life—theatres, riding, dancing and fencing lessons, demands for extra sums of money to pay his bookseller—a serious worry. He knew the cost of money; he had slaved for his. It is hard to smile at the rather pitiful reaching out in his letter of the 29th of May 1803 when after begging Henri to be a little careful he turns to his own cherished schemes. 'Je me mets en forte mesure pour établir à Claix des mérinos de Rambouillet. Il nous seroit très important que tu fisses ce dont je t'ai prié dans ma dernière lettre. Tu ne m'en a pas dit un mot . . . il me faut un berger; que ce berger soit élevé à Rambouillet; que je tire un lot de brebis de Rambouillet; que je tâche surtout d'avoir un bélier du premier degré. Si ce n'étoit pas si loin, j'irois moi-meme prendre les renseignements indispensables. Tu devrois bien m'en éviter l'embarras. . . .' Much his lively intelligent son cared about the merits of Rambouillet merinos and Chérubin Beyle's craving to make money out of his estate. Did he do as he was asked? Probably not. He was too full of himself, too exalted, too happy.

He had matured. Good company, charming women, friendliness in the air, excited him to talk, he talked well, with enjoyment and wit—and an incautious frankness. But in order to feel safe in a Parisian drawing-room, among intelligent and perhaps illustrious persons, he needed the reassurance it gave him to be well turned-out, every detail correct. Remember how young he still was, how incredibly vulnerable through every sense. To be shabby mortified him. When his allowance did not come his pride or his vanity suffered; and he hated his father bitterly for what he took to be meanness. Writing to Pauline on 26 February 1805 about a day he called the most splendid of his whole life, he says: 'Enfin tu connais ma laideur: des femmes que j'ai offensées me firent compliment sur ma figure. J'étais en bas, culotte, gilet noir, habit bronze, cravate et jabot superbes. Hein! suis-je fat de te conter cela, mais je pense tout haut avec toi.' He charmed at these times because he was not showing off; he was simply himself and content to be himself, and as willing to listen as to talk.

There was a reverse side to his mercurial gaiety. One or two people may have known, later, that he was deeply and incurably diffident. A few women certainly knew. He rarely gave himself away, but he was as quickly and easily run through by the perhaps imagined contempt of a person he respected as if he had no defences. At that level he had none.

His most intimate friend at this time was Félix Faure. Three years older than Beyle, he passed for a worldly cool-headed young man, more mature than his contemporaries, but the letters he wrote Beyle were filled with youthfully exalted sentiments about country walks and the beauty of a calm sensible life; he read a great deal, listened to music, and had a proper appreciation of good wine: he is more moved than Beyle by the tragedy of that young smiling Victorine Bigillion, who had become violently insane and was in a cell with a little straw for a bed, and nothing on her but a blanket.

Without any open break, their friendship came to a bad end. In October 1804, Faure is writing, 'Je t'aime de tout mon cœur,' and later trying vainly to persuade Beyle to use his chance, through the Darus, to get on: 'Tes parents Daru paraissent destinés à aller à tout; n'es-tu point tenté de t'accrocher à leur fortune?' After 1814 and the return of the Bourbons he saw his own chances very clearly and took them. He climbed coldly and ruthlessly: in 1832 the most blackguardly of kings (Stendhal's epithet for Louis Philippe) made him a peer. In a bitter paragraph in *Brulard* Stendhal speaks of his 'égoisme et une absence complète de la plus petite étincelle de générosité . . . le plus plat de tous mes amis et celui qui a fait la plus grande fortune', lumping him with Édouard Mounier ('un plat, adroit et fin matois') also now a baron, as 'formerly my friends'.

A few others of his Grenoble schoolfriends were in Paris, including the two Louis', the loyal and indispensable Louis Crozet and Louis de Barral. His lighthearted affection for Barral lasted, unaltered, to the end of his life. He cannot have shared any of his deep interests with this amiable character who lived contentedly with the charming young woman Beyle had pressed on him, and after some twenty years married her. He loved in Barral, or so I think, a carelessness and simplicity he might have cultivated in himself had he, like Barral, been the son of an indulgent, wealthy and well-bred father. In the *Souvenirs d'Égotisme* he remarks that Barral has become a miser; it does not seem to have disturbed him: hearing about the marriage he sends a message: 'Est-elle comtesse, la chère Annette? Mille tendresses à ce nouveau ménage.'

He frequented various salons, perhaps more welcomed at this time as a lively talker than as an intimate. He dined with the

Darus. The elder Daru was dead. Pierre had married the nineteen-year-old Alexandrine Nardot, a handsome young woman, good-humoured, sensible, lively, who bore him eight children in twelve years. Without going so far as to forgive, still less trust his un-reliable young cousin he was willing, within reason, to be on civil terms with him. After a little more than a year in Paris, Beyle went back to Grenoble. He had debts: the letter he wrote his father in May 1803 lists these, or some of them, and suggests ingenuously that if he came home for four or five months now he would save enough money to see him through the winter in Paris, where the many invitations he receives run him into a great deal of expense; and, too, he has not seen his beloved family for a year: he will need to buy some clothes before coming, and—'Si tu es en argent, j'y ajouterais une vingtaine de volumes qui me seront très utiles à Claix pour travailler. . . .'—without cynicism one can believe that the debts had more to do with his plan than family feeling. But he had a strong love of the hills and lime trees of Claix and, as instinctive in him as any of his passions, a recurrent need of solitude. In the event he stayed for ten months in the Dauphiné, and during the summer worked tranquilly at Furonières. He was back in Paris in the spring, in the rue d'Angivillier: but towards the end of the year moved to more presentable lodgings where he could put up his Gagnon uncle during the splendours of the coronation. He viewed these coldly enough himself; his juvenile worship of the victorious young general of 1796 was in eclipse at this time. There is more than this to be said about his feelings for Napoleon, but let it wait.

He was working, he worked ceaselessly. Subjects and themes for plays trod each other down in his mind, comedies, a tragedy in five acts, a fresh aspect of *Deux Hommes*; he studied them as he studied and dissected friends and acquaintances; analysed them back to first principles, wrote, rewrote. He cultivated his theatrical friendships. He was a passionate partisan of Josephine Duchesnois against her younger and beautiful rival Mlle George. Mlle Duchesnois was a celebrity and immensely talented; she had splendid eyes and a well-shaped body, but was otherwise ugly:

allowed to visit her, he might, if she had paid him more than the casual interest given to a young admirer of no useful importance, have imagined himself in love. Instead he took lessons in elocution, partly to get rid of what he calls his provincial drawl; first from the tragedian La Rive, then, in December, from Dugazon, younger, livelier, and a successful teacher.

Here, among the pupils, he met Mélanie Guilbert, and fell into one of the real but not one of the deeply disturbing and consuming passions of his life. He was nearly twenty-two and she nearly twenty-five, the younger daughter of a modest middle-class family in Caen. She had brought with her to Paris a child she had had when she was twenty and had placed her with foster-parents in Neuilly, and was living on the very small capital left her by her father. Except for her obstinate will to succeed in the theatre she had no notable qualities, and few as an actress. Beyle endowed her with every heroic and graceful quality of mind and spirit, and approached her with timid carefulness not to alarm or offend. He knew exactly how to seduce a woman; he had studied the method as a military commander prepares a battle, as a mathematician resolves an algebraic equation, or as he himself studied the art of writing a comedy, by the rules. He had the strategy at his finger-tips. And, when his heart was involved, was too diffident to apply it, even had it been better than a comic mask of the real Beyle, impulsive, spontaneous, lovable. If anything inclined Mélanie to him during the first weeks of their acquaintance it must have been the youthful clumsiness and sincerity he strove to hide. She was the more experienced and her lessons had been harder, and she was, in her way, as sensitive as the young man courting her with such fatuity.

He had other schemes on his mind at this time, more weighty in so much as they had to do with making money, but not safe from the glances of the Comic Spirit; this kept an eye on him throughout the whole of his life, only withdrawing, humbly, in face of the final perfection of the *Chartreuse de Parme*. He was not a Beyle for nothing: he believed in his genius, in his intellect, in the rightness of his theories; he believed that as the son of a member of the *haute bourgeoisie* of Grenoble he was sure of inheriting a competence. In the meantime he must live. Since he returned from Grenoble he had been thinking seriously of a career in banking or commerce. Surely he could make enough money to enjoy a civilised life—his idea of civilised living derived from both Gagnons, uncle and grandfather—and have time and energy to go on preparing himself to become poet or dramatist? In his perplexity he turned for advice to a Fortuné Mante who had been at school with him, and from the Polytechnique had gone into commerce. He now became one of Beyle's dearest friends, reliable, charming, the best head he knew, a financial genius. They spent months debating his problems. Beyle drew up plans; sensible enough but for their fatal likeness to Chérubin Beyle's carefully reasoned schemes for making his fortune: like his they seduced just because they had been thought out step by step: the flaw was in the assumption that he had faced what was involved in an apprenticeship to banking and was prepared to take it seriously in practice. Moreover he misled himself or was misled about his father's wealth: he saw nothing out of the way in counting on an eventual loan of thirty or forty thousand francs to establish a Maison Mante, Beyle et Cie.

Mante himself was going to Marseille, to the firm of Charles Meunier, colonial importers. Beyle's plan to follow him might, like so many of his projects, have been left hanging indefinitely in the air if at about the same time Mélanie had not accepted an engagement in the theatre in Marseille. This decided him: he could not let go of her, and a letter from Mante about the shakiness of the Meunier firm and the difficulty of finding openings in commerce made no impression on him. He went with her to see her child in Neuilly, and a few days later travelled as far as Lyon with her. Here he left her to finish her journey alone, and went off to Grenoble to talk to his father and grandfather. His schemes offended both of them, and after two months of mortifying argument he got nothing except a promise to go on paying him his allowance in Marseille and an offer, negotiated through family friends, of an unpaid post with Meunier.

He left Grenoble in July 1805, travelling down the Rhone in a decrepit boat from Valence to Tarascon, a three days' trip; thence by coach to Marseille. Mante, in his rôle as hero's friend, had taken a room for him in the hotel where Mélanie was living: four days later the long drawn-out siege of a town which perhaps had only been waiting to be invested ended in her bed. It is all absurd, yet there is something young and timid and enraptured about it, something he remembered thirty years later when he added her name to three others as one of the great passions of his life.

For a few months he was completely happy. He spent all his free time with her. On evenings when she was not acting, he coached her energetically in her rôles or—besotted young man—in Destutt de Tracy's logic and philosophy. One Sunday he had the exquisite pleasure of watching her slender body standing naked in the clear water of a stream shaded by great trees, reminding him of a painting he had seen as a boy, three women bathing in just such a stream, which had filled his immature body with a shocking ecstasy.

His mind was less vulnerable and direct than his heart; it had protected and amused him with myths since his childhood, and always would do, and when he told Dr Gagnon that he was the father of Mélanie's child he was inventing a long happy past spent with her as well as seeking to persuade his grandfather that the relationship was a serious one. Writing to Pauline in September about his happiness and Mélanie's sublime nature he begged her, if he were to die, to look after his daughter.

Apart from Mélanie, and apart from fitful efforts to work at *Letellier*, there was nothing satisfying about Marseille. The work he did was not only dull, it had no future: he was in effect a minor clerk, and it did not take him long to realise for himself that the firm was in an invalid state. Towards the end of the year he was briefly engaged in a scheme to form an association with a Parisian banker, a M. Flory. Between them, he and Mante would have had to provide a hundred thousand francs. This mirage flickered out. And his early idealising of Mante had soured: at close quarters in Marseille he not only was an intrusive third, but was showing himself naked of all the virtues, charm, great intelligence, Beyle had invented for him in the first months of their intimacy, turning out to be cold-hearted and a pedant, in short a bore, the one fault Henri Beyle never forgave man or woman. When he left Marseille he was very happy to lose sight of a friend he had once thought of as the right husband for his dear Pauline.

Any one of his worldlier friends would have expected him to tire as quickly as he did of life as a clerk in a provincial city, and of a mistress, charming, sweet-natured, with no intellect to speak of, no temperament, a mediocre actress. Perhaps she was too sure of him to notice that she was ceasing to enchant, or too kind to him. The three other women with whom in memory he compared her, two of them well-born, the third a whore, had one quality in common: they made him suffer.

In his letters to Pauline he hid his disillusion: it would have mortified him to admit it. As it turned out, the break with her was made easy. She was not a success with Marseille audiences, not earning her salary; with a good conscience he could advise her to go back to Paris and friends she had there who could help her. She left Marseille at the beginning of March. She had sensibility and courage, more courage than talent. When, in May, she was offered an engagement in Naples she wrote him a very simple, delicate letter, asking him to tell her whether she was still loved and wanted. Whatever he found to say in reply, he did not re-assure her.

After she had gone he had one of his rare moods of revulsion against the instability of his life. He summed up his exasperation with Marseille crudely. 'Paris, auditor, huit mille livres, repandu dans le monde du meilleur ton, et y ayant les femmes.' Not a very exalted ambition, but he was not in the habit of arranging his motives in any better light than he saw them at the time.

Nothing else, nothing on the credit side? Yes, a vein of the finest ore. His sister was one of the few persons in his life against whom, for as long as he could think of her as the companion of his heart and mind, he had no impulse to guard himself. The letters he wrote her, many of them enormously long, show a passionate concern for her—'. . . toi la bien-aimée de mon cœur'. . . . 'Je t'aime de toute mon âme, je n'aimerai jamais de maîtresse autant que toi. . . . Je te forme, tu es la fille aimée de mon cœur'. . . . He is writing to a loved sibling: more precisely, to an imagined feminine part of himself, eager to share with her the thing he valued most: knowledge and understanding of life itself. He was still sending her lists of authors she must get by heart, and expounding them lengthily, Condillac, Hobbes, Saint-Simon, Marmontel, Vauvenargues, Pascal, many others: memoirs, philosophy, and, above all, logic. So deep a part of his own happiness and security rested on his passion to learn, that he could not conceive she would not be steadied, and her life, like his, enriched, given point and meaning, by the same things. 'Je compte beaucoup sur la *Logique* pour te rendre heureuse,' he told her.

No other woman drew such letters from him, a heady compound of learning, wit, and love. But they were written to a young woman who did not exist except in the image he made of her. In letter after letter from Marseille he advised her, and very sensibly, on the conduct of her life as a marriageable young woman. Less wisely, in his lively anxiety to pass on to her in good time his own experience, he warned her to guard herself against trusting anyone. Sincerity with those you love, yes, but in the world one must never forget the need for a mask. 'Apprends à être hypocrite. . . .' It is hardly likely that the not very intelligent young woman he was writing to understood what she was being told, about life or about Henri Beyle.

She did not write to him very often, not nearly often enough to content him: 'Je t'aime bien, mais je souffre cruellement quand tu restes ainsi deux mois sans m'écrire. . . .' In one form of words or another he told her so in many of the letters of this time, with as little understanding of her needs and nature as she, in her boredom and simplicity, of his.

Outbreaks of rage against his father, at best reckless, mar some few of his letters at this time. No doubt Chérubin Beyle, a proper Dauphinois (as one says: a proper Yorkshireman) was a harsh character, and without charm or noticeable warmth: he was obsessed with schemes in which he tried to interest his resentful son, consulting him about the house he was building in Grenoble, clumsily anxious for the young man to approve of the panelling: in the same letter he wrote at length of his plans to buy Swiss cows and a magnificent bull: to rent a mountain near the farm to pasture a herd would cost a lot of money, but bring in enough to make things easier financially for the family. What does Henri think? Henri's thoughts about his father, poured out to Pauline and Dr Gagnon, are indecently harsh: there is no meanness or vileness of which Chérubin is not capable, even to letting his children die of hunger if their grandfather dies before they have laid hands on a little money. A sharp rebuke from Dr Gagnon had no effect: the aversion Chérubin's son felt for him, allowed himself to feel, had little to do with any reasons; it was as primitive and ritual as that between two species of animals.

He had begun his efforts to get back to Paris two months before Mélanie left Marseille, by writing to his grandfather for advice. Only too eager for him to get out of a low commercial life the family rallied to him at once. The obviously right thing for him at twenty-two, rising twenty-three, was a place in the administration; and the only person who could help him was Pierre Daru, now conseiller d'État and advancing rapidly in the Emperor's favour. Dr Gagnon wrote to him with impeccable tact, assuring him that Henri had grown up, was sensible, hard-working, sobered by his experience in industry, thoroughly to be trusted; and Romain Gagnon wrote very shrewdly to Martial Daru. It is a pleasure to watch the delicate skill with which, in their polite prose, Henri's whole career since he threw away his commission becomes a self-education in worldly wisdom.

Pierre Daru's response to the pressure of the family could have been and no doubt was expected: he had no illusions about his young relative's change of heart, and no belief that he had ceased to be better than unreliable, either politically or as a young man it would be profitable to advance. He behaved with superb reticence and made no move to help.

Restless and impatient—when was he ever able to wait patiently on events?—Beyle could not bear to hang about in Marseille. At the end of May he left and went to Grenoble, with nothing promised. He stayed there a month and, rather pitifully, a flicker of warmth sprang between father and son, perhaps the first, probably the last. Then, in July, he left to go back to Paris, turning aside on the way to visit his friend Louis Crozet in Plancy-sur-Aube, the dull little village some twenty miles from Troyes where, now an engineer in the Ponts-et-Chaussées, Crozet was constructing a canal lock.

The poor fellow was in a desperate state. He had fallen deeply and clumsily in love with Blanche Rougier de la Bergerie, the oldest of the three daughters of the Préfet of the Aube. His case was completely hopeless. He was not only very unattractive, he was in debt and shabby. In his misery the only comfort he had was the angelic kindness shown him by Blanche's youngest sister: 'la divine Jules', he had called her in his despairing letters to Beyle, 'la plus tendre et la plus spirituelle des femmes'. His acute intelligence, his good sense, had not entirely foundered, he could still discuss books and politics and a brief encounter in Auxerre with Madame de Stael, but he talked obsessively about his unhappiness. Ah, if only he had a private income, if he were only a sous-préfet, if only he could marry Blanche and have Jules as a sister-in-law. No doubt Beyle was sorry for him, and no doubt, too, he was repelled and bored by outbreaks of anguish that jarred on his fastidious reticence about his own griefs and mortifications. After two days of it he left, to go on to Paris.

Chapter 5

PIERRE DARU WAS civil, in his formidable manner, even friendly, and in no hurry to do more for the repentant prodigal than show him the cool hospitality he would have shown any not very important member of the family. Henri was too diffident to ask questions. He waited, and kept himself in view. In the meantime he was content. He had Paris, a furnished room and his books and notebooks in the rue de Lille, friends—Félix Faure, the Rebuffels, mother and provocative daughter, and Martial Daru, whose very suitable wedding he attended in September—and at the Théâtre-Italien a company singing the *Matrimonio Segreto*: he had not lost, never did lose the delight in Cimarosa he had given himself up to in Italy at seventeen. Other simpler pleasures fell into their places. Mélanie, waiting to make her début at the Comédie-Française, took him back: she had too little vanity—she might have been a better actress if she had had more—to go on punishing him and herself. He was no longer in love, but he had a genuine feeling for her. She was very likeable.

Discreet family pressure, and Martial's insistent advocacy, brought Pierre round. In mid-December, when Martial left Paris to take up his official post in Germany, he took Beyle with him in his carriage. They reached Berlin at the same time as Napoleon. At the end of the month Pierre, now QMG of the Grande Armée, signed Beyle's nomination to the *commissaires des guerres* as provincial assistant and despatched him to the occupied province of Brunswick, which Martial was to administer.

Confirmed in his appointment a month before his twenty-fourth birthday, and entitled to wear the uniform he had envied his friend Edmond Cardon seven years ago in Paris, he acted as Martial's personal assistant, carrying out his duties with efficiency and zeal. There is no doubt that he could have been successful in government service. 'J'ai tombé avec Napoléon en avril 1814,' he says in *Brulard*. But Napoleon's fall was not the decisive turning-point: the fault, in a geological sense, was in himself, in the quarrel between the passion of the scholar and writer and the instincts of shrewdly practical forebears.

He worked hard and he enjoyed himself. There were plenty of opportunities in an aristocratic society amusing itself and the occupiers with receptions, balls, dinner-parties. He hunted in the Hartz forest, shot partridges, hares, deer, and smaller animals, squirrels. And more important for his other life, for the man to come, he heard Mozart, for the first time. As time went by, and without dislodging Cimarosa, Mozart became the composer closest to him on the level where both of them discover the anguish at the heart of happiness. There are passages in the *Chartreuse* which one is tempted to say that only a Mozart among novelists could have written.

Naturally he fell in love, less a serious passion than a poignant liking for a young woman he met through his intimate and lasting friendship with a man twelve years his senior, Friedrich-Karl von Strombeck, adviser and steward to the Grand-Duchess Augusta-Dorothea, the only member of the ducal family who had chosen to remain in the occupied province. Wilhelmine de Griesheim—Mina, for Beyle, when he is recalling the ten or so women who have filled his life—was twenty, a beauty, singularly graceful, charming, and poor. It was not a love-affair, not even a flirtation, she was too well-bred, and too simple and good, for anything of the sort, as he had the sense and grace to realise. She left Brunswick when her father refused to serve under Jérôme Bonaparte and was exiled. Nothing had happened, nothing could happen, but he remembered her with a rare gentleness.

Naturally, too, he had a mistress, a comfortable Charlotte Knabelhuber whom he could enjoy without any responsibility except to hide the liaison from her wealthy Dutch protector. And there was an unexpected visit from Mélanie, travelling through Germany to join a French acting company in Russia. She lunched with him, went on her way, and—this is something too much of an *opéra-bouffe*—in Moscow married an unattractive Russian general, whom she seems to have left behind when she fled in 1814.

He travelled a good deal in the course of his duties. Long vivid letters reached Pauline from Metz, Munnerstadt, Berlin, Schoenebeck, Basse-Saxe, Strasbourg, with, as always, complaints of her failure to answer. 'Ton confesseur t'a-t-il défendu de m'écrire?' But what could this inexperienced not very perceptive young woman have made of such a letter as that of 26 March 1808 with its recollections of their childhood, of his young delight in the line of the mountains round Grenoble, of the exquisite pleasure of a light touch evoked in memory?

This year, 1808, his life, with the departure of Martial to Spain, changed radically when he was put in charge of the imperial domains in the department of the Ocker, four districts. Overnight he became an important man, addressed, by a slight stretch of his official status, as Monsieur l'Intendant, a senior administrative officer of the Quartermaster General's staff. He carried out his greatly enlarged functions with complete confidence and success. Writing to Pauline in May he spoke with frank pleasure about his new eminence. A youthfully sincere letter, but with an undertone. 'Il y a quatre ans, j'étais à Paris avec une seule paire de bottes trouées, sans feu au cœur de l'hiver, et souvent sans chandelle. Je suis ici un personnage: je reçois beaucoup de lettres dans lesquelles les Allemandes me disent *Monseigneur*; les grands personnages français m'appellent *Monsieur l'intendant*; les généraux qui arrivent me font des visites . . . je vais à des dîners de cérémonie, monte à cheval, et lis Shakespeare; mais j'étais plus heureux à Paris. Si l'on pouvait mettre la vie où l'on veut, comme un pion sur un damier, j'irai encore apprendre à déclamer chez Dugazon, voir Mélanie dont j'étais amoureux, avec un mauvais redingote. . . . Mais que de moments délicieux dans cette vie malheureuse! j'étais dans un désert où, de temps en temps, je trouvais une source; je suis à une table couverte de plats, mais je n'ai pas le moindre appétit.' A mood, yes. But more than a mood, a ripple from a deep restlessness. Would he, even if Napoleon had not fallen, have changed course again? It is possible, but not certain. He might have gone on to become a peer, a high government official with academic and literary leanings—but no *Le Rouge et le Noir*, no *Chartreuse de Parme*, no *Vie de Henry Brulard*. It is not certain. Nothing is certain with Henri Beyle.

Starting on 1 February 1808 he carried on an immense official correspondence with provincial ministers, with préfets, with generals, with Monsieur l'Intendant Général Daru himself. Scattered through the mass are letters to Pauline before and after her marriage to François Perier-Legrange. But one looks in vain in them for any reference to the death on 6 April of 'ce caractère élevé et espagnol, mon excellent grande tante Élizabeth Gagnon'. (Epitaph written for her in 1835, in *Brulard*.)

In November he was transferred to Paris. His duties during the four months he spent there were obviously not heavy, and his rank allowed him to enjoy the best restaurants, good seats at the theatre and the opera, where he listened with deepening under-standing to Mozart. He read, he took fencing lessons, he had a pleasant social life. At the end of March he was ordered to report to Strasbourg as one of the *commissaires des guerres* attached to Pierre Daru, now the Comte Pierre Daru.

Nine days later, as part of Daru's staff, he left for Vienna. The roads were a disorder of infantry struggling to get forward, cavalry, pack horses, ambulances, walking wounded, convoys, guns; some towns had been badly knocked about in the recent fighting, and the dead were still lying in the streets. Writing in May 1809 to Félix Faure, still a close friend, he told him: 'J'eus réellement envie de vomir . . . en voyant les roues de ma voiture faire jaillir les entrailles des corps des pauvres petits chasseurs à moitié brûlés.' Daru drove him even more savagely than his other aides; during the days spent in towns arranging for supplies, finding horses, seeing to hospitals for the wounded, he scarcely slept. On the road he could sleep in his carriage; and now and then, in an inn, he found a willing bedfellow. He was living at a pitch of energy and excitement even he seldom reached, and he forgot nothing, none of the sights and sounds; thirty years later, when he needed them for Fabrice at Waterloo, they were still fiercely alive in his mind.

He reached Vienna, or rather Schönbrunn, on 13 May, more than a month after leaving Strasbourg; a few days later Martial Daru, appointed to administer the city and province, asked to have him transferred to his staff. Removed from his terrible elder cousin, he was free, in what leisure he had, to enjoy Vienna. There were pleasures: women, music. In June, eight days after Haydn died, he attended the performance in his honour of Mozart's *Requiem*, sitting well in front, in full uniform. He did not care particularly for the *Requiem*: on the other hand, *Don Giovanni*, given at the theatre most weeks, in German, was becoming that one of the operas he would go to any trouble to hear: it moved him as did certain lines of his beloved Vergil: *Sunt lacrimae rerum et mentem mortalia tangunt.* . . .

He was not at the battle of Wagram on the 6th of July, not even, as in *Brulard* he implies he was, in his capacity as *adjoint aux commissaires des guerres.* He may have got himself there later but, on the day of the battle, when Martial Daru and his staff were there evacuating the wounded to hospitals in Vienna he was lying in bed with what, writing to his sister, he called a severe attack of fever. He heard the guns. He speaks in *Brulard* of having a 'vérole horrible', whatever that may mean: a recurrence, perhaps, or a sequel of the infection he had been treated for in Milan in 1800: the term 'vérole' was used indifferently for gonorrhoea or syphilis.

He had a brief affair with a girl about whom we know little more than her name—Babet. Much more serious, he was now absorbedly in love with the Comtesse Daru, Pierre's young wife, one of his half self-inflicted half real infatuations: it had begun to sprout when he was in Paris, and now he had every temptation to persuade himself that he loved and was loved. They were the same age, twenty-six. It fell to him to act as her escort in Vienna; he took her to the Kahlenberg and they looked down together at that incomparable view, Vienna and the Danube, the heartland of Europe. His journal is full of his trepidations and the conduct of his siege of her. Between his timidity and her unaffected friendliness she did not yet realise his state, and he was still some way from the moment at which he might have declared himself when towards the end of November she went back with her husband to Paris.

She was not his only preoccupation during these months. Three years ago his highest ambition had been: 'Paris, auditor, huit mille livres. . . .' He had been immensely thankful to accept much less, but the taste of a life of gaiety and comparative security and, perhaps, his intimacy with Martial Daru and Faure, climbers both, had its influence on him. Already in October he was writing to Pauline about a faint chance of promotion to the Conseil d'État as auditor: by the time, mid-January, when he left Vienna for Paris, the chance had become an absorbing possibility: nothing, he believed, stood between him and the start of a new and distinguished career except his lack of the private income, seven thousand five hundred francs, an auditor must have. Naturally he saw it as his father's duty to settle it on him, and pressed him impatiently. Without abnormal delay, Chérubin agreed, and Henri Beyle was in the list of new auditors published in August: later the same month, also on Comte Daru's recommendation, he was further appointed one of two inspectors of Crown furniture in the palaces of Versailles and Fontainebleau, with the task of making an inventory of the Emperor's works of art.

As always, he told himself to advance over the ground he had won. His next move should take him to a barony, and for that he had to be the possessor of an entailed estate: his father must settle property on him. He wrote and had others write urgently to Chérubin, and sent Félix Faure to talk to him. His letters to Pauline are involuntarily comic in their desperation: with a title he has chances, even matrimonial chances not now in his reach; without it he will certainly end up as a sous-préfet in some miserable provincial hole. Chérubin must hand over land, borrow on it, sell part of the Claix estate. But Chérubin had already done all he could do, he had debts and mortgages: he did not refuse outright, nor did he do anything. What sparks of tolerance his son may have had for him flickered out altogether. He did not let the project drop, not at once, perhaps not entirely until 1813. By that time he had more tangible troubles and excitements.

His greed for social success at this time is real. It was an ambition as far as you like from his ambition to be the greatest of poets. But need we make fools of ourselves by looking for excuses for him, for the smilingly assured creator of Fabrice and Julien? It may be true that he tried for elegance and social honours because he was acutely conscious of his clumsy body, lack of money, and provincial background, but there is more to say. Let it lie for the moment.

During these two years before 1814 he passed easily enough as a young man about Paris, witty, cultivated, a brilliant talker. He had his office in the hôtel Châtelet and a salary of eight thousand francs. His duties, even allowing for the occasional tasks laid on him by Pierre Daru, were not heavy; he had time to enjoy possessing eighteen waistcoats and twenty-seven shirts with jabots, two servants, a carriage and a gig, and lunching in the newly-opened café Hardy while his gig waited at the door. If an acquaintance thought him a conceited ass for it he was unmoved. He spent freely, bought a great many books, and for the only time in his life ran seriously into debt. He had a charming apartment shared with a friend, Louis de Bellisle, and a mistress. Angélina Béreyter was a young actress singing minor rôles at the Théâtre-Italien; he pursued her for six months before she became a sweet-tempered comradely bedfellow, joining him every night after the theatre. He was not in love with her, she was a pleasurable habit, kept up until he left Paris, for good, as he thought, in July 1814.

In a superficial light the portrait seems to be that of a young man with more energy and vivacity than good sense. That this was not the opinion of colleagues of the standing of the Duc de Broglie, the Comte Amédée de Pastoret, and the Comte d'Argout —the last a member of an old and aristocratic Dauphinois family —is very evident from their readiness, at a later time, when he needed help, to try to give it.

Among the salons open to him were several that any

determinedly ambitious young man would have cultivated with particular care. Henri Beyle was incapable of making friends whose only merit in his eyes was that they were important or useful. When he made friends it was out of affection, amusement, respect, never out of calculation. Taken by Louis de Bellisle to call on Madame Beugnot, he recognised very quickly that he could trust both her worldly knowledge and her friendship. He presented himself at the Darus every day, not out of tact and not only because he was still stubbornly in love with Mme Daru, but because there he felt himself part of a family. Through his friend Crozet, still miserably building his dam in the Aube and suffering the pangs of rejected love, he came to know the Rougier de la Bergerie family, mother and three daughters, now living in Paris. Although of the three he preferred the 'divine Jules', he did not take a great deal of notice of this young woman who later, sixteen years later, became his cherished friend for the rest of his life. She was on the point of marriage, and became Mme Gaulthier that same year.

Although Pierre Daru's wife figures in the *Vie de Henry Brulard* as one of Henri Beyle's four great loves, and although she possessed his imagination and a noticeable part of his thoughts for two years, it is difficult to believe that his failure to persuade her to take him seriously caused him any but a quite manageable grief. If grief at all, infinitely less poignant than the cry wrung from him when, over fifty, he was writing about his life: 'Clémentine est celle qui m'a causé la plus grande douleur en me quittant. Mais cette douleur est-elle comparable à celle occasionné par Métilde qui ne voulait pas me dire qu'elle m'aimait?'

In 1810 Alexandrine Daru was an elegant twenty-seven, matured by child-bearing, sensible, gay, frank. No doubt by now she had realised that the young man's devoted attentions were not cousinly, but no woman, however sensitive, could have had any idea of his exaltations and tactics, or failed to be touched by his involuntary diffidence, the youngest thing in him. Quite apart from his infatuation he had a simple and real affection for her, as indeed she had for him. If the record he kept of his campaign is correct it was not until the end of May 1811 that he attacked. She deflated him with gentle firmness: he did not accept defeat and she had to speak coldly. He was taken aback, but was he, except in his confident trust in his strategy, wounded?

He could be fatuous, but he was not a fool, and not simple, and he was driven by a purpose which at his most injudicious and absurd never ceased to nag him. Even now he was not contented by the life he had coveted and in fact enjoyed: he read Cabanis and Tracy's *Logique* again and made efforts to work on *Letellier*, neglected since Marseille, and tried and failed to get himself sent on a mission to Rome. The pressures on him to continue in what he calls a life of high favour were formidable, but would he, without the débâcle of 1814, have succumbed to them?

Unexpectedly, perhaps prompted by his wife, Daru now offered him a short leave.

Seen off by Félix Faure and a tearful Angélina, he left for Italy by the early morning coach: Milan, the Scala, and that Angela Pietragrua whose image, after more than ten years, still held him. It was a nine-day journey: he arrived in the evening of 7 September and hurried to the Scala, moved almost to tears.

With Angela his happiness was chequered, running between doubts of himself and ecstasy. She was as seductive and voluptuous as he had remembered her. He told her that eleven years ago he had been crazily in love with her. 'Why on earth,' she cried, 'didn't you tell me?' As maladroit as always when he was deeply caught, his behaviour now must have puzzled and bored her. Her own strategy was simpler: she allowed him to see her, to visit her in her box at the Scala, shed a few tears over him and told him that it would be better if he left Milan. It might, he reflected, be tactically sound to withdraw temporarily: he agreed to go, and on the morning of 21 September, the day he was due to leave, she surrendered. He made a discreet note on his braces of the hour of his triumph, and twelve hours later left for Florence and Rome.

Martial Daru was in Rome *en poste*, living in the Quirinal. He saw to it that Beyle met the right people, took him to call on Canova and other respected artists, and certainly told him that Comte Daru had become Secretary of State, news which ought to have sent him straight back to Paris with his congratulations. If the thought entered his mind he easily ignored it: he spent five days visiting galleries, churches, the bird-haunted ruins of the Coliseum, then Naples for six days, disappointed by the music he heard there, and again Rome, briefly. He returned to Milan to find that Angela was away, staying in the country: he made the mistake of following her, and was angrily rebuked for compromising her with her husband who was, she told him, jealous. Was he taken in? She packed him off to visit the lovely Borromean Islands in Lake Maggiore for two days: when he returned she forgave him, made an appointment with him for midnight and broke it. Back in Milan, she played him like a fish she had no wish to land. She ordered him to allay her husband's suspicions by going to Venice. This time he refused. During the hours when she would not receive him he sat in the room he had rented for their meetings and read Lanzi's *Histoire de la Peinture en Italie*. It fascinated him, and he was seized by the idea of translating and making use of it for a work of his own.

At last, in mid-November, he forced himself to leave. Even now he did not go directly to Paris, but spent some days with Pauline and her husband on their estate near Grenoble. When, three months after the start of his leave, he presented himself for duty, he was enormously surprised to discover that he was in disgrace both with his new chief, the Duc de Cadore, and with Daru. He was left out of the promotions and awards of decorations at the end of the year, and it was several weeks before Daru brought himself to recognise his existence, and then only because of his wife's persuasion. There is no profit and no return in kind to be got from advancing a young man who has every quality making for success —energy, wit, brains, practical competence, charm and the rest of it—except the instinct to succeed.

In the winter of 1811–1812 the country was tired of seemingly endemic war; people were growing apprehensive and bitter. The atmosphere in Paris was one in which even Henri Beyle might have found it difficult to concentrate on his personal preoccupations. His official duties were not without interest, and he took them seriously: witness his detailed reports to the Duc de Cadore on his inspections of Fontainebleau and the Louvre. But within a week of returning he had begun to make drafts and notes for the vast study of Italian painting, sculpture, architecture, he had conceived in Milan, and he worked on it, completely absorbed, for some five months, until the middle of May, before becoming restless. Auditors to the Conseil d'État had the privilege of acting as imperial couriers: he applied to be sent to Russia with despatches, and in July went off with two enormous portfolios and fifty packets, including a letter the Empress gave him personally for her husband.

After an execrable journey: 'Tout est grossier, sale, puant au physique et au moral. . . . Je vieillis,' he wrote Faure from Smolensk, he reached Army Headquarters and Pierre Daru on 14 August, and Moscow, on Napoleon's heels, a month later. The fires began that night. After a day or two Daru and his staff were forced to move out of the city. It was being well and truly pillaged, and as Beyle left he took a volume of Voltaire from the library of an abandoned great house; it was one of a set bound in red morocco, the one entitled *Facéties*, an odd choice, and in the circumstances suitable enough: afterwards, in the Retreat, he felt some remorse for having mutilated the set, and dropped the book in the snow.

Several days later they moved back to the blackened half-ruined city: he found decent lodgings in the Academy of Medical Sciences, and seized the chance of a feverish liver attack to work on *Letellier* and make notes for his history of Italian painting. He read Rousseau's *Confessions* and came to the conclusion that their author's misfortunes were due to his ignorance of the principles of pure *Beylisme*. On the day he arrived in Moscow he had searched the burning city for Mélanie without finding her: now he was told that she had left before the fires, and he wrote to a common friend in Paris that she could have his apartment in the rue Neuve-du-Luxembourg, and asking him to see her safely installed there.

He believed he was going to spend the winter in Moscow, but he was under the orders of the QMG, and to his intense annoyance—'j'ai resisté comme un diable . . . on m'a fait une réponse que ma plume se refuse d'écrire,' he wrote a fellow-auditor—he was given the task of ensuring for large reserves of food, requisitioned or to be bought, in the governments of Smolensk, Mohilev and Vitebek, and on the 16th of October he left: he had with him some three hundred men, a convoy of fifteen hundred wounded, a large sum of money, and a raging toothache. Harassed by parties of Cossacks they took over two weeks to reach Smolensk; one night was passed in the certainty of being massacred at daybreak: writing later to Faure he said it had been worth coming to Russia for the experience of that fortnight alone. He had a volume of Madame du Deffand's letters—where did he get it?—and read it on the march and during the icy discomfort of the weeks in Smolensk. He was able to distribute three days' supply of rations for the whole army, almost all it had between Moscow and the disaster of the Bérézina. Against the cold there was no provision: in the Retreat when an exhausted man fell it killed him as he lay, as it must have killed a young Gagnon, Romain Gagnon's son, last seen in Wilna, 'pleurant et regrettant sa mère', by Pierre Daru. Daru gave the boy his last horse and his last pair of boots, but somewhere between there and Kovno he disappeared.

One of the two young fellow-auditors who had shared Beyle's room in Moscow told Mérimée, years later, that he had owed his life to the calmly brutal insistence with which Beyle forced him, half dead with fatigue, to cross the Bérézina before the uncontrollable flood of stragglers overran the bridges. Beyle himself reached Wilna on the 7th of December, fifty days after he had left Moscow. He was back in Paris on the last day of January, numb and exhausted.

He hoped for some official recognition of his services, a place, or a decoration. He got nothing, not even the *croix bleue*. The two auditors who had been in Moscow with him, including the one he forced over the Bérézina, were made préfets. Probably, when Daru had no further use for him, he could expect to get something:

in the meantime he went back to wrestling with a recalcitrant *Letellier*. And cultivated his friendship with Mme Beugnot. All he wanted, since he could not go to Italy, was to live quietly in Paris.

In April, barely recovered, he was sent off to the army. He reached Bautzen in Saxony in the middle of the fighting and made the discovery he later passed on to Fabrice del Dongo, that it is impossible to form a coherent image of a battle while it is going on. In the course of the next few days and weeks his mind threw off its lethargy; something of the excitement of the journey from Strasbourg woke in him: it was as much a physical as an intellectual emotion, and he suffered a relapse when, an armistice signed, he was made administrator of the province of Sagan in Silesia. It was a dull place; he was overworked and very bored and, as he was apt to do when bored, he fell ill, but seriously, succumbing to an influenza epidemic as deadly as the one that raged through the bored English army in the spring of 1919. After sick leave in Dresden, Daru sent him back to Paris, where he was told to take a couple of months in the Midi. Inevitably he went off to Milan instead, writing to Pauline not to give him away and reminding her to harry their father about the barony—that guttering candle, soon to be snuffed out.

Angela was on holiday some seven miles from Milan, at Monza; he hurried there at once. She received him kindly. The brief entry in his Journal—'One spoils happiness by describing it'—is all he allowed himself. His habitual reticence—a phrase, a few delirious words, as at the end of *Brulard*, about moments of intense happiness or pleasure—was part of the impulse to guard himself, a deep mistrust, learned very young.

The next day, appeased, he went back to Milan. He spent some more or less contented days with her, but when she returned to Monza he was not encouraged to follow her. Instead he went to Lake Como for four days: then a day at Monza, two years to the day since he recorded a note on his braces; then Milan again, alone. To distract himself he read Molière and added to the notes he had been making in the margins of his edition for several years.

He was purely happy only at the Scala. During his last fortnight in Milan Angela was indulgent: he might have stayed with her longer, but he was hoping to get himself posted to Italy and he decided not to try the patience of his masters.

He reached Paris on 30 November 1813 in the middle of a worsening military and political crisis: the allied forces were closing in. He was excused conscription and sent off to Grenoble with the Comte de Saint-Vallier, himself a member of an aristocratic Grenoble family, to prepare the defence of the Dauphiné. No loving Gagnon grandfather welcomed him. That 'camarade sérieux et respectable' of his childhood had died on the 20th of September, when Beyle was at Lake Como, dreaming about Angela and admiring the view.

He had been handed a maddening and exhausting task. He worked desperately, organising the national guard, amassing supplies of arms and food for the region. A ludicrous fraction of his difficulties was due to the attitude of his fellow-citizens, characteristically inclined to jeer at the claim to authority of an energetic young man no better than themselves: nothing worse than ironical smiles and comments, mockery, and quarrels with a timid and deliberately unhelpful préfet, but exasperating and wounding. The military situation was hopeless. In March Saint-Vallier withdrew to Valence. Beyle went back to Paris. With Louis Crozet, picked up on the way, he got there in time to watch the departure of the Empress and her young son. The same day he tried and completely failed to persuade the director of the Musée Napoléon to put the more valuable paintings in a place of safety.

During the following days of confusion and suspense he walked about the city, snatching up every detail of the disaster: he was in Montmartre when the Russians occupied the Butte. His personal, like his official, life was in ruins. The Conseil d'État was dissolved, he no longer had a position, and thirty thousand francs worth of debts. Nor was Pierre Daru, his own career disrupted, in any mood to advise or help him.

There were items on the credit side: in the past eight years he had learned an infinite deal about human nature, the vanities of rulers and the resentments, cowardice, and courage of the ruled: no writer, no novelist, ever had a finer education: more important, the mind and nerves exposed to it were incomparably sensitive, an instrument of superb delicacy. Items not of immediate profit.

He took the one step he could to establish a narrow margin of security. On the 7th of April, as an official of the dissolved Conseil d'État, he notified his formal adhesion to the provisional government, that is, to the Bourbon régime. Sensible—and a long step from the child exulting in the guillotining of Louis XVI, 'un des plus vifs mouvements de joie que j'aie éprouvés en ma vie', and devouring with his eyes (his phrase) the regiments of dragoons marching through Grenoble on their way to Italy in 1792. Did it discomfort him to see his acceptance of the Bourbons published in the same issue of the *Moniteur* (12 April) as the notice of the abdication of Napoleon? A twinge? A wry self-mocking memory of the delighted ten-year-old regicide? He had no moral reason to regret the fall of a dictator. He was neither a rallié like Chateaubriand, actively in favour of the return of the Bourbons, nor yet actively anti-Bourbon; and it was not at this moment unreasonable to expect that the restored family would ride the country on a freer rein than the fallen Emperor.

It was difficult, Mérimée wrote after his death, to know what he felt about Napoleon. Not, at this distance, difficult to simplify the most ineffaceable experience of his life—most ineffaceable, not most passionate. There is the rebellious child, hating 'bourgeois, Jesuits and hypocrites of every sort', calling himself a Jacobin and idolising the conquering young general. In common with a million of his countrymen the seventeen-year-old dragoon in Milan is 'fou de Napoléon', the hero who incarnated liberty and was making France the master of Europe. That was 1800. Four years later, when the revolutionary general had himself crowned, he reverted instinctively to the view he summed up in a note made later on in a copy of the *Mémoires d'un Touriste*: 'Napoléon sauva la révolution en 1796 et en 1799 . . . et il eût mieux valu pour le bonheur de la France qu'il fût tué en 1805 après la paix.' Set beside that: 'Les guerres de Napoléon ont été extremement belles et un peu utiles. . . . La vieillesse de ceux d'entre nous qui ont vu la retraite de Moscou ne sera pas ridicule.' (*Promenades en Rome*, 1828) And: 'On ne peut plus aimer un autre général après avoir vu agir Napoléon. On trouve toujours dans les propos des autres quelque chose d'hypocrite, de cottoneux, d'éxagéré, qui tue l'inclination naissante.' (Preface to his incomplete life of Napoleon) And: 'Napoléon (que toujours j'adorai) . . . ' words written by the horribly bored consul in Civitavecchia in 1832.

It is in *Le Rouge et le Noir* that his deepest most lucid feeling about Napoleon blazes.

He was bodily and nervously tired. Between anxiety and his restless running about he fell ill and spent the second half of April in bed with symptoms of pneumonia. He was resting his hopes of employment in the new administration on his friend Mme Beugnot, whose husband had become Minister of the Interior in the provisional government, and—it was not an unreasonable idea —might get him posted to the embassy in Florence. While he waited, he set himself to translate a book he had read in Milan, a pedantic work on Haydn by an Italian librettist called Carpani. He worked over it, adding original comments and judgements, and clarifying the ideas. To a point, it was a first rough sketch of his manner in later books of criticism or memoirs, sharp descriptive detail, anecdotes, vivid evocations of place and character, smilingly ironic argument. It was much more a reckless plagiarism of the Italian author. With the lightest heart, not to say light fingers, he omitted to give Carpani any credit. Then, to make a longer book, he added a short life of Mozart drawn largely from a pamphlet by Winckler, enriching it with a few of his own infinitely more informed and perceptive opinions, and two letters on Métastase, also drawn from existing studies. He signed the patchwork Louis-Alexandre-César Bombet. True, his animation of Carpani's lifeless book created something it is still possible to read with a degree of pleasure: the original would long ago have become dust. Not an excuse for larceny but, for his readers, a mitigation. Add that he gained nothing by it. Published in January 1815, uncorrected, full of errors, the book was an all but total failure: of the thousand copies printed not much over a tenth were sold: the printing had cost him 1,790 francs paid to the publisher, and he lost more than a third of the money. Some time in 1816 Carpani discovered that he had been pillaged, and wrote bitterly to the *Constitutionnel*. His letter drew a mocking reply from Bombet, perhaps written by Crozet. The poor Italian's further complaints received the same teasing insolent treatment: Bombet was in effect a character in an unwritten novel, and Henri Beyle, by now in Milan, felt no responsibility for his misconduct.

In 1814 he had other things on his mind. With his close friend Louis de Bellisle, like himself one of the swarm of solicitors for a place, he spent the greater part of his evenings in Mme Beugnot's salon. His friend was, he believed, his rival in Mme Beugnot's affections, and Bellisle did in fact get a place quickly, as *maître des requêtes*. In May Comte Beugnot moved from the Interior to the Police, another set-back to Beyle's chances. He began to think seriously about Italy, Milan or Naples, where living was a great deal cheaper than in London. Did Beugnot, as in *Souvenirs d'Égotisme* Beyle says he did, offer him an important post as food controller for Paris? It is not obviously improbable. His proven competence as administrator in Brunswick and his war record in Russia and Grenoble qualified him for such a post: his resentment that his services had received no recognition was natural enough. He goes on to say that out of reluctance to serve under the Bourbons he refused the offer. 'Je ne sollicitais rien. . . . L'extrême mépris que j'avais pour les Bourbons'—he is writing in 1832—'c'était pour moi alors une boue fétide, me fit quitter Paris peu de jours après n'avoir pas accepté l'obligeante proposition de M. Beugnot.' But in fact, in 1814 he had been willing if not anxious to be employed. His sincere loathing for the returned Bourbons came later, when the new régime had had time to reveal itself as not only reactionary but dull, heartless, a despotism meaner than Napoleon's, a reign of petty terror and delations, personified for him in 1821 by: 'Le gros Louis XVIII, avec ses yeux de bœuf, traîné lentement par ses six gros chevaux, que je rencontrais sans cesse.' What is strictly true is that he got nothing, no place, though in July Beugnot had apparently decided to recommend him for a consulate somewhere in Italy. But by this time he had decided to go to Milan.

Possibly his influential friends, even, for all her genuine affection for him, Mme Beugnot, mistrusted the restless brilliance of a not always politic suppliant. Not by nature a suppliant, and concealing, or deluding himself that he concealed, a deep confused reluctance to commit himself. His doubleminded restlessness may have been more obvious than he knew. Had he been patient he would certainly have got something, but he was running out of patience, or beginning to be angry. Who knows how much, behind his witty talk, his vivacity, he felt diminished by being passed over, and wanted to turn his back? He seemed to himself to be thinking about it sensibly and coolly. His decision had been arrived at by a process of reason; he could defend it lucidly in argument. It was not an abrupt idea: as early as April he was reflecting that he could live very cheaply on a fourth floor in Rome. To set off against his debts he had only the sale of his possessions, carriage, horses and the rest, and 16,000 francs left him by his grandfather. He expected to go on drawing his half-pay as *commissaire des guerres*, arranged for when he was made auditor: on that, and a small annuity bought with Dr Gagnon's legacy, and a modicum of help, not to be counted on, from his father, he could live in Milan and write. And surely M. Beugnot could get him appointed to an Italian consulate as easily in his absence as if he were hanging about in Paris? All of it logical reasons for going, and as such irrefutable: there is no denying logic. Reasons that masked a born distaste for being held down. Masked the ecstasy of a boy riding into Milan on a morning in spring. On another level, the deepest, his decision was made by a Beyle obsessed by a craving to make up for the time he had lost and to do it in a country he thought the loveliest on earth. Add his unassuaged passion for a woman he was not sure of.

To his friends, his decision to go away was another proof of unreliability, irresponsibility, innate frivolity. Mme Beugnot was certainly offended by it. Certainly, too, it destroyed what chances he had of a solidly prosperous life. Later he reflected, nonchalantly enough, that he could have been rich and respected: 'Que de belles occasions j'ai manquées. . . . L'activité des demarches necessaires pour amasser 10,000 francs de rente est impossible pour moi. De plus il faut flatter, ne déplaire à personne. . . .' True enough, as true then as today, and his refusal or, to be more precise, his careless neglect of the need to climb tirelessly and discreetly, to court the right people and opportunities and the rest of it and the rest of it, had no moral undertones. Though he may not even have realised or thought of it in these terms, he was as temperamently incapable of keeping a steady eye on the main chance as of enduring boredom. He wanted success and recognition. It is not simply that he was unwilling to pay the price for them: to all effect, he overlooked the necessity. There was not an ounce of genuine calculation in him. Calculations, yes, strategies, plans, rationally worked out to a not invariably rational end, and directed to an immediate desire. His sole lasting desire was to write a masterpiece—'Le vrai métier de l'animal'. And this is not the way to worldly success. On the contrary. It is a form of madness, and by its narrowly pure vision infinitely likely to miss success as, in his lifetime, he missed it.

Would he, safely established in a préfecture or a peerage, have written the *Chartreuse*? Most unlikely.

Writing, in April 1835, from exile in Civitavecchia, to the friend he trusted more than anyone in the world, he protested, '. . . mais je crève d'ennui. Le vrai métier de l'animal est d'écrire un roman dans un grenier, car je préfère le plaisir d'écrire des folies à celui de porter un habit brodé qui coûte huit cent francs.' One need not accept every judgement he passed on himself, but this is final. It was the meaning, the worth, the profound *leit motiv* of his life and being. Everything else is deeply irrelevant.

Chapter 6

H E R E A C H E D M I L A N in the second week of August 1814 with four thousand two hundred francs in his pocket, determined to live on five hundred francs a month. He wrote an engaging letter, signed Dominic, to Mme Beugnot, reminding her to try to get him some modest diplomatic post in Italy; then turned to working on the Italian painters, to sitting, ravished, in the Scala, and to his first arguments with the Pietragrua.

The *Histoire de la Peinture en Italie* had been planned as a vast work, covering painting, music, and the country itself, its natural beauties and the determining influence of its climate and soil on the character, manners, and genius of its people. He helped himself from a great many sources and transmuted the whole by the immediacy of his perceptions, judgements, reflections, flashes of wit. He had a superb visual memory. He could draw on years of reading in allied subjects; and he revised and recast endlessly. In essence what we get from him about his chosen painters is a complex and lucid statement, sensible even in paradox, never boring, of their effect on an acute sensibility, an acute intelligence, against a background of light thrown across the thickets, social, moral, aesthetic, in which every generation (including its artists) struggles to think and act. Probably an intelligent art critic today finds it profane, even indecent, that Henri Beyle looked at a great painting very much as though he were listening to an opera, alert to seize the effect on his own mind of the 'sublime vistas' he saw in Poussin or the distances he admired in Corregio: they pierced him to the heart in the entranced moments before his attentive intellect took charge. Of this book he wrote to Louis Crozet: 'Je le dédie aux âmes sensibles'. Let us leave it there.

It was never completed. He published two volumes, largely on Florentine painting. The third part, on painters of other schools, remained as notes and drafts, enriching later books, *Rome, Naples et Florence, Promenades en Rome,* and the eternally readable *Mémoires d'un touriste.*

Milan seduced him again: the music, the simplicity of manners, the spontaneity and lack of vanity of the ordinary Milanese. He was overwhelmingly thankful he had come—'Mon Dieu! que j'ai bien fait de venir en Italie,' he said again and again. Had he been able to trust Angela he would have been completely happy.

Possibly he had arrived when she had more absorbing amuse-ments: he had hardly passed three nights with her when, on the palpably false excuse that his countrymen were unpopular in Milan, she ordered him to absent himself for at least two months. He protested, and full of jealousy and mistrust obeyed her, and spent six weeks in Genoa and Florence. Back in Milan, he had to put up with her petulance and bouts of ill-temper. Did he, as he told Crozet later, think seriously of killing himself? I strongly doubt it; ideas for future books were swarming in his head, and he had too solid a conviction of unused powers to waste them. What-ever he says, the desperately hard work he did during these months was not in any real sense a refuge from despair; it was the satisfaction of a craving.

So were his visits to museums and picture galleries and, above all, the Scala. Every evening he spent there was a delirious happiness: the insidious intoxication of opera and ballet, and the familiar delight of talking, as in a well-found salon, to attractive women and distinguished visitors to Milan. He does not write about music as might a composer, a virtuoso. Why should he? He is neither. His ear was sensitive and acutely retentive. When he writes: '. . . la musique, quand elle est parfaite, met le cœur exactement dans la même situation où il se trouve quand il jouait de la présence de ce qu'il aime; c'est à dire qu'elle donne le bonheur apparement le plus vif qui existe sur cette terre', the phrases are precise. The music he preferred gave him the same overwhelming delight as certain landscapes or as the smoothness of a woman's skin. The reveries it induced in him are one of the more subtle of sexual pleasures, an interior and extreme point of sensation, involving nerves, senses, imagination.

The part reveries played in his life is of singular importance in the effort to see a little deeper in him than his involuntary frankness with himself, sincerity, gaiety, acute sensibility, passion for lucidity. He was fifty-three when he wrote, in *Brulard*: 'Je vois que la rêverie a été ce que j'ai préféré à tout, même à passer pour homme d'esprit.' It is as true as most of the things he tells us directly about himself, not a vast number, for all his apparent frankness—viewed in retrospect his reticence is formidable. He would have found it difficult or impossible to say at what age he fell into a habit at which he became an adept. Imaginative and erotic forms of a child's memory of a lost tenderness and security, reveries were his deliberately, even if unconsciously, willed refusal to accept the reality of disappointments, rejections, failure. They were a source, welling up in him to his last days, of his indomitable happiness. And inseparable from his genius, a thread in the same creative energy as the infinitely complex and controlled structure of the *Chartreuse de Parme*.

Early in the new year Angela tried to persuade him to go to Grenoble. He got as far as Turin. There he heard that Pierre Daru's wife had died giving birth to another child, her eighth in twelve years: she was thirty-three. His grief was real, the sudden sense that he had lost true affection, true kindness, not the phantasma of an aristocratic mistress. 'C'était après toi la meilleure amie que j'eusse au monde,' he told Pauline.

Back in Milan, he got himself a cheap lodging near the Scala. What better did he need? He was content. 'Dans les beaux temps de mon goût pour la musique,' he says in *Brulard*, 'à Milan de 1814 à 1821, quand le matin d'un opéra nouveau j'allais retirer mon libretto à la Scala, je ne pouvais m'empêcher en le lisant d'en faire toute la musique, de chanter les airs et les duos. Et oserai-je le dire? quelquefois le soir je trouvais ma mélodie *plus noble* et *plus tendre* que celle du maestro.'

Who with any feeling for him will not cherish the delicious image of Henri Beyle, thirtyish, already putting on weight, walking lightly back to his room, glancing at the score in his hand, humming, singing?

In March the news reached Milan that Napoleon had landed in the Golfe Juan. If there was a living spark in the ashes of his youthful enthusiasm it gave him no trouble. He felt no impulse to rush back to France, still less to Grenoble, which had opened its gates willingly to the returned Emperor, or to involve himself again in the life he had lived during the last years in Paris. He was thirty-two, very poor, and working with intense concentration. And, with his deplorable inability to guard himself against the violent motions of the most uncontrolled of hearts, he was more infatuated with Angela than ever. In July she agreed to spend four or five days with him in Venice. He was to go ahead and wait for her in Padua. She failed to turn up, and, bored, he went on without her, lost courage, and hurried back to Padua. She came, and was kind, and he was happy. How long, for the sake of the intoxicating pleasure she could give him, would he have gone on persuading himself that she was not deceiving him, not simply a deliciously engaging whore? In his *H.B.*, the memoir published, tardily, after Beyle's death, Mérimée repeats a somewhat scabrous story Beyle told him about the end of the affair, so ridiculous that it is probably true, not worth inventing. Whether, told of his misfortune by Angela's maid, he did or did not one day watch himself 'being betrayed a few feet from his hiding-place,' a small closet into which the maid had shut him, he certainly broke with her abruptly, at first exhilarated by his freedom, then, for some months, regretting her bitterly.

During these first years in Milan he was often ailing, fever, palpitations, giddiness, and had to be bled and blistered. Perhaps they were simply bodily disorders, perhaps they were what nowadays, for want of sharper insight, we call easily psychosomatic. His anxieties were real enough: the failure of the War Ministry to send him his half-pay income as *commissaire des guerres*, his debts in Paris, and what he felt as his father's miserly treatment of him. Oddly enough, in view of his extravagant way of life when he was an auditor, he disliked having debts; he had always seen himself getting a préfecture or some other high appointment and able to clear them. He owned a house in Grenoble, one which Chérubin Beyle had built at a corner of the place Grenette and had handed over to him, heavily mortgaged, as a gesture towards helping him to a barony. He decided to go to Grenoble and discuss their father's situation with his sisters and their husbands. He stayed there some two months and returned to Milan in June having done little more than cast a distrustful glance at the morass of Chérubin's speculations and borrowings. He sold the house after his father's death; the details are confused and dull, but he **was** able to pay his Parisian creditors.

Straitened though he was, he led a satisfying life. This year, 1816, he discovered—'grand époque pour l'histoire de mon esprit', he wrote to Crozet in September—the powerful *Edinburgh Review,* and began making handsome use of its authoritative literary and critical pages. He stretched his income to travel in Italy. He adored travelling. It was, after falling unluckily in love and hearing Mozart, his liveliest pleasure. 'J'aime les beaux paysages, ils font sur mon âme le même effet qu'un archet bien manié sur un violon sonore; ils créent les sensations folles; ils augmentent ma joie et rendent le malheur plus supportable.' (*Mémoires d'un Touriste*) He had other pleasures: in his friends' boxes at the Scala and in the most distinguished salon in Milan where his host, Monsignore de Brême, received the leaders of liberal society and every foreign visitor of note, his witty tongue and experience of the world were an asset. He met Byron here. Excited by him, by his fame, his looks and aristocratic hauteur, he talked with reckless brilliance about Napoleon and his own relations with the Emperor. 'I am sure that Beyle is to be believed,' Byron's travelling companion, Hobhouse, commented afterwards, noting it all down for use.

Later—in 1825—he lent one of Byron's books to his young friend Victor Jacquemont, who discovered scrawled in the margin of more than one page the sentence: 'Lord Byron est un duc, un fat, et ne parle jamais que de lui,' and wrote him a taunting reproof.

He was nearing the end of his strenuous efforts to complete the two volumes of the *Histoire de la Peinture*: he needed the money he confidently expected it to earn him. He had been sending the manuscript to Louis Crozet in Plancy-sur-Aube, to be deciphered —his handwriting is atrocious—criticised, corrected, annotated and sent on to the publisher in Paris, Didot, and the proofs read and the rest of it. Enormously long instructions came with each batch, new passages to be inserted, others rewritten, revised, amplified. 'Je n'ai pas voulu t'assassiner de lettres,' he wrote to Crozet on 15 November 1816, but he did—save that Crozet was a willing victim, as willing, acute and capable as always. His misfortunes and disappointments had not softened him: he had become vainer, narrower in his personal outlook, caught up in the pettiness of provincial life, more touchy and aggressive. No doubt there was a trace of vanity in the devotion he put into helping his friend, and why not? Who else would have done so much? Their intimacy at this time was perhaps as deep and close as they ever came to complete confidence in each other, without very much warmth. Crozet served and without understanding judged Beyle, and Beyle was as aware of his old friend's fine intelligence and intuitive sagacity as of his surly intolerance. Crozet married this year, a cousin: years later Beyle blamed her for their having grown apart: he should have blamed the early withering of Crozet's hopes, and his own rebellious happiness even in defeat.

Between early December and February he spent six weeks in Rome studying Michelangelo's consummate paintings, an overwhelming emotional and moral experience: the last long instalment to reach Crozet was the passage on the *Last Judgement*, described by Delacroix, not given to politeness, as a 'morceau de génie', but minor corrections and modifications went on into May.

The printing and distribution at his own expense of the volumes stood him in close on four thousand francs. Spattered with misprints, they came out at the end of July. Financially it was a disaster. In seven years, of the thousand copies printed only a quarter had been sold. It took him twice that time to pay off

Didot. The one pure satisfaction he got out of a book which on and off had obsessed him for five years was the visit paid him in a hotel in Paris by Comte Destutt de Tracy, to whom he had sent a copy. Such was his reverence for the author of *Idéologie*, read with passion in his shabby room in the rue d'Angivillier in 1802 and taken up again and again since, that he was tongue-tied. Or so, writing about the event fifteen years later, he says. It is quite likely. He could be very shy when he was moved deeply.

For all his anxiety to get the *Histoire* off his hands, he had not only taken time during the past year to make notes on the art of comedy, that not yet wholly quenched ambition, but had put together a second book, so various, so lighthearted, you could suppose it cost him no effort. Its kernel was the notes he had been making of his Italian travels for years, intending to use them some time, in some form. Since the bitter disappointment of his first weeks in Paris and his rebirth in Milan at the age of sixteen, his love of Italy had become that of an experienced adult for the mistress he knows as well as any human being can know the bodily and mental reality of another, however intimate. *Rome, Naples et Florence en 1817* is a comedy of improvisations, reflections on the Italian character, on his reading, on music, lively anecdotes snatched up with both hands, imaginary encounters, superb descriptions of places, passages borrowed—that should read appropriated—with slight acknowledgement or none, from the *Edinburgh Review* and other sources (these include Goethe and, despite his rasping criticisms of her, Mme de Stael), put together to evoke the image of a country he knew as familiarly through his senses as through observation and study: 'J'éprouve un charme, dans ce pays-ci, dont je ne puis me rendre compte: c'est comme de l'amour; et cependant je ne suis amoureux de personne. L'ombre des beaux arbres, la beauté du ciel pendant les nuits, l'aspect de la mer, tout a pour moi un charme . . . une sensation tout à fait oubliée, ce que je sentais à seize ans, à ma première campagne.' To write the book amused and refreshed him. Produced, in September 1817, by Egron, printer to the Duc d'Angoulême, and signed by M. de Stendhal, *officier de cavalerie*, it brought him in a profit of a hundred francs more than it had cost him: he spent part of it on buying the collected volumes of the *Edinburgh Review*. It was the first time he used the name we know him by as writer, but not as friend, *homme de société*, consul, lover: it is probably a recollection of the little town of Stendal, in Saxony, through which he passed on official journeys during his years at Brunswick between 1806–1808: it lies between Brunswick and Berlin. And also the first time he had made any money by writing. There was also a second French edition printed in London, by a Soho firm, and sold by the enterprising Henry Colburn. And an English translation the following year, printed by the same firm and published by Colburn, so that there may have been a little more money for its author, in this edition the Count de Stendhal. Dear Beyle.

This year saw, too, the beginning of his intimacy with the Baron de Mareste, an old casual acquaintance who now became and remained for the next ten or twelve years one of his closest friends. You could not have called it a marriage of convenience, yet it oddly resembled the familiarity possible between two intelligent and companionable adults, one of whom is content to act as the other's devoted aide. Beyle's long lively letters to Mareste from Italy about the interests they shared, music, art, politics, are filled as well with demands for services of all kinds, made as of right and amiably met by Mareste. He was of constant use to Beyle during this time: that does not account for the closeness and warmth of a friendship which Beyle later—and disingenuously, but he was provoked—describes as *estime mais non amitié*.

Pauline's husband had died in the previous year. She had been left badly off, and he spent October and part of November 1817 in the Dauphiné helping her to sort out her confused affairs. Impossible, in the melancholy half-denuded chateau, to avoid catching sight of two spectres passing and repassing. In his endless youthful letters he had talked a great deal about their living together later. On 12 July 1804: '. . . je crois que tu n'auras jamais de meilleur ami que moi; lorsque nous serons vieux, nous pourrons nous réunir et passer huit mois à Paris et quatre à Claix. Si le hasard me donnait quelque fortune, j'en achèterais un petit château près de Milan, pays délicieux, à Canonica, sur l'Adda, entre Milan et Bergame.' And, two years later, 22 March 1806, from Marseille: 'Écrivons-nous, ma bonne ami: nous sommes l'un pour l'autre nos meilleurs amis. . . . Lorsque nous serons dégoûtés du monde l'un et l'autre, nous prendrons une petite maison à Paris, où nous passerons notre vie ensemble et en attendrons la fin dans le sein des beaux-arts et de la plus tendre amitié.' And less than two years before her husband's death, writing on 3 December 1814 from Milan: 'J'ai grand intérêt à ta santé, car j'espère que nos affaires s'arrangeront de manière que nous pourrons passer ensemble notre vieillesse.' Whether or not he broached the idea during these weeks, it must have crossed his mind.

He had other preoccupations, his missing half-pay, and in Grenoble their father's latest attempt to ruin himself by building a new road across land he was developing. In November, to get away from the gloomy chateau, brother and sister fled to Milan. Here he established Pauline in lodgings alone, rented a box at the Scala for her, and went back with relief to his engrossing life in the city he loved better than any other place on earth: much older, exiled from it, he had only to recall it for an adolescent to interrupt him with a cry of pure love—'Je suis arrivé à Milan en 1800, j'aime cette ville. Là j'ai trouvé les plus grands plaisirs et les plus grandes peines. . . . Là je désire passer ma vieillesse et mourir.' His days fell at once into a familiar pattern: long hours of work— he had taken up again his fortunately never finished life of Napoleon—reading, strolling, talking with literary and political friends. From seven o'clock to midnight he was at the Scala, listening, score in hand, and talking his way through a round of the boxes. He was a passionate admirer of the ballets devised by the choreographer Salvatore Vigano, ranking him with Cimarosa as one of the greatest geniuses of the age. He was happy. He once told Mareste that except in Paris and London there was no conversation. There was always his own.

At some moment in the first weeks of 1818 he fell in love again, with the suddenness of a lightning-bolt. Mathilde Dembowski—

to himself he called her Métilde—came of a family of the *haute
bourgeoisie* of Milan, the Viscontini. Her marriage at seventeen to
Jean Dembowski, twenty years her senior, a Polish army officer, a
naturalised Italian, had been a disaster; Dembowski was dissolute,
jealous, brutal, and in 1814 they separated. She was twenty-seven
when Beyle was presented to her by one of his friends among
prominent liberals: she was herself a firm liberal. She had beauty,
great dignity, calm—and high principles. Henri Beyle was in
love with one woman or another during most of his life, in-
corrigibly, deliberately, uncontrollably, happily, unhappily, and
none of his fevers racked him so mercilessly as the one with which
she infected him. No fibre in his mind or body was untouched by
his useless passion for her. Writing fourteen years later, in *Souvenirs
d'Égotisme*, he still cannot bring himself to talk about it. 'Peut-
être un jour, quand je serai bien vieux, bien glacé, aurai-je le
courage de parler des années 1818, 1819, 1820, 1821.' For the rest
of his life there was a region of his mind he had only to brush
against for the pain and ecstasy to claw him: none of his novels is
unmarked by it.

Not long after his first meeting with her he had to go back to
Grenoble with his sister, and he spent a boring four or five weeks
there struggling with the lawyers about her finances. She had not
inherited enough to live on. She would have to be helped. Faced,
now that there was nothing to prevent it, with the possibility of
having her to live with him, he felt only dismay at the prospect of
being saddled with a companion he had outgrown as irrevocably
as he had outgrown the ingenuousness of the young man writing,
'Répond-moi, donc, mon petit, toi la bien aimée de mon cœur.'
His revulsion was spontaneous. On a deep level he had become as
avid of solitude as of music, travel, sensual satisfactions.

A man less careless of opinion, or vainer, would have erased the
callous paragraph he wrote about her in *Souvenirs*—'. . . cette
huître ennuyeusement attaché à la carème de mon vaisseau, et qui
bon gré mal gré me rendait responsable de tout son bonheur à
venir'. What is more, he never ceased to feel responsible for her, a
feeling that can outlast softer emotions. He would do anything he

could for her except live with her. He willed her all he had to leave, and one of the first things he did as soon as he became a consul was to give her a pension of seven hundred francs from his meagre salary.

He went back to Milan without her.

Métilde was away. In her absence Milan was a dead city: he spent hours of the day obsessed with his image of her. Her coldness when she returned dejected him without opening his eyes to the fatuity of hoping that his besotted state would move her— except, as it did, to distaste and boredom. Neither during the years in Milan nor later was he able to understand her behaviour. He beat his brains to discover the cause of it, even at moments trying to persuade himself that she forced herself to be harsh because she was fighting against a weakness for him. To a woman it is obvious that she felt something very near physical repugnance: her behaviour shows every mark of it. He was heavy; he had lost much of his hair during the savage cold and privations of the retreat from Moscow, and wore a toupet. Mme Dembowski was not one of the women who, drawn to him by his gaiety, his exquisite sensibility, his ironic wit, forgave or did not notice his ungainly body and quite shocking intelligence. Possibly the imprudence of his talk offended her as later it offended the Comte de Tracy, striking her as ill-bred or frivolously provocative and dangerous. When, seldom enough, he was alone with her, his timidity made a tongue-tied wretch of him.

He was very unhappy. But to the end of his life there remained in him, in nerves and senses as responsive to a touch as the strings of a violin, an ineradicable excitability and gaiety. He did not enjoy the Scala less because Métilde made him suffer: it was during this time that he took the operas of the young Rossini to his heart. He spent days or weeks in the country near Milan, writing to Mareste from Lake Como of its ravishing beauty and the pleasures of life there. So cheap, too: he had a delightful room overlooking the lake, and in the evening the gayest and freest of company. If *le Bâtard* (his father) left him no more than thirty-four thousand francs he would be rich for life here. In Milan he seized every

84

chance offered him to spend his evenings in informally friendly houses where he probably talked too much and too indiscreetly. There was a charming young widow, the Comtesse Cassera, whose box at the Scala he enjoyed visiting, and with whom he had supper and played cards. There was Salvatore Vignano's daughter Elena: she was young, in her mid-twenties, beautiful, an admirable pianist, and a singer whose exceptionally pure voice became fuller, livelier, as she sang. He spent three or four evenings in the week with her and her circle of friends, from eleven until two in the morning, listening to her, enchanted. At the time it did not occur to him that reports of his social habits reaching Métilde convinced her of his incurable levity.

He could be fatuously clumsy with her. There was an occasion when, shortly after she had left Milan on a visit to the old Etruscan town of Volterra, he followed. Only the attendant Comic Spirit can have known what he hoped would come of plans which involved wearing green spectacles, discarded at the wrong moment. The sincere despair of his reply to the icy rebuke she sent him may have touched her; she seems to have made him some sort of promise to see him in Florence on her way home. He went there at once, and waited for six weeks, writing her immense letters, explaining himself, asking forgiveness, asking mercy, talking of his past, trying to rouse her interest in him. The last, short, begging her to write to him to Bologna, ends very simply: 'Je suis bien malheureux, Henri.' Did she write? Almost certainly not. No one can be more unkind, and indifferent to her own unkindness, than a woman bored by a devotion she finds exasperating, even ridiculous.

There were other letters waiting in Bologna for him, telling him that his father had died more than a month earlier. He can only have been vastly relieved. In spite of anything he had seen in the last years of his father's confused speculations in land and other property, this *fils de famille* had always believed and been actively encouraged by his grandfather to believe that he would be left well off. A legacy of ninety or a hundred thousand francs, the least he expected, would bring him in an income of some nine thousand francs, not a great fortune, but enough for him to live in modest ease, and study, write, travel.

He reached Grenoble in August, and was roughly disillusioned. Chérubin Beyle had made a failure of everything he touched; his desperately hard work, his schemes, his whole life, a failure. He had died heavily in debt. At a distance, his defeat has its pitiable side.

His obdurately unloving son did not immediately realise the extent of his misfortune. Writing to Mareste from Grenoble, he told him that thirty or forty thousand francs was as much as he would get from *le Bâtard's* estate. It was a wildly exaggerated guess. After some four weeks of wrangling with his brother-in-law, his younger sister's husband, he was out of patience, and rashly abandoning his interests went off to Paris, leaving creditors, lawyers, and the family to settle the affair between them.

Mareste had taken a fourth-floor room for him in the hotel in the rue de Richelieu where he was living himself. The hôtel de Bruxelles was run by a M. and Mme Petit, formerly in aristocratic service as valet and lady's maid. M. Petit's impeccable manners, scrupulous honesty and precise rather old-fashioned sense of his position delighted Beyle, and so far as his perplexities allowed it he was content. He debated his prospects with himself. Should he, if it were even barely feasible, go back to Milan, or should he force himself to what, when he was writing to inform Pierre Daru of Chérubin Beyle's death, he called 'le pénible métier de solliciteur'? He dared not think of losing Métilde. She had written to him, very briefly, to Grenoble, no doubt a letter of condolence. Mme Dembowski was nothing if not well-bred. Naturally he had replied at length, trying for calm. But at the end the crying of his heart broke through. 'Je finis ma lettre, il m'est impossible de continuer à faire l'indifférent. . . . Adieu, Madame, soyez heureuse; je crois que vous ne pouvez l'être qu'en aimant. Soyez heureuse, même en aimant un autre que moi.'

In the end, after having stayed a little over a month in Paris, and taken no steps about finding employment, he went back to Milan.

Métilde greeted him very coldly. His letters had vexed her, and she refused to see him more than once a fortnight. He stood for long hours watching her windows to catch sight of her shadow on a curtain.

Towards the end of that year, December 1819, he started the book published two and a half years later as *De l'amour*. Begun as a form of thinking about Métilde, of evoking, exploring, inventing, imagining, in effect living his obsessive passion for her, it is a chaotic book, in places moving, in others brilliantly analytic, paradoxical, subtle—and planless: the witty brain, the pulses of the heart, tear it apart between them. The writing was, in the beginning, itself an obsession: he made notes for it at home, in boxes at the Scala, on playing cards in a salon where he was spending the evening. But it is not an uncontrolled outpouring: his will to recall lucidly, candidly, with absolute sincerity, and without vanity, the follies and affections of his heart justify words he allows himself to write in the first part of the book: 'Je fais tous les efforts pour être *sec*. . . . Je tremble toujours de n'avoir écrit qu'un soupir quand je crois avoir noté une vérité.'

Supreme saying—to be burned into the brain by self-respecting writers.

The book was more or less finished in July. To save time and money he did not have it copied, and in September handed the manuscript to an Italian friend to post from Strasbourg to Mareste, who was to see to its printing in Paris. Thereafter it vanished, for more than a year.

As the weeks passed with no sign of it, he became mortally anxious and depressed. He could never put together this one of his books from the mass of indecipherable notes which was all he had. He made attempts to work on *Letellier*, that spectre still moving spasmodically in his brain. Nothing came of them. His health was giving trouble; he had the first twinges of gout; earlier in the year he had had a sharp attack of gonorrhoea, the first for more than ten years, he assured Mareste. He travelled a little, Bologna, Mantua.

That summer what he felt as the worst blow of his life fell on him. An anonymous enemy denounced him to his friends in Milan as a French government agent and he found himself being avoided. At almost the same time the police began to watch him as possibly a dangerous character, a revolutionary. To be mistrusted both by the French consul in Milan and by the police as a violent liberal, and cold-shouldered by his liberal friends themselves was an irony he would in other circumstances have enjoyed analysing.

Mareste and Crozet advised him very strongly to leave. He hesitated for months, not able to face the anguish of losing at a stroke Milan, the Scala, the enchanting countryside, the lakes—and an unrelenting Métilde. Though he had given up hope of her she possessed him, his senses and imagination, as cruelly as ever. In January, whatever illusions he may have been cherishing about his chances of continuing to live in Italy as writer, scholar, amateur of music and the arts, were killed by the news from Grenoble that when Chérubin Beyle's massive debts were paid and his sisters given their share of what remained, his income in future—counting the nine hundred francs of his uncertain military pension and the annuity, some one thousand six hundred francs, bought with his grandfather's legacy—would be less than three thousand francs. There was nothing he could do except return to Paris and try for a place, but it was another two months, longer, before he asked Mareste to find out from his cousin, Comte d'Argout, what sort of post he could apply for with a reasonable hope of getting it: Apollinaire d'Argout, his colleague on the Conseil d'État, whom he considered a dull fellow, had been well-disposed to him then. 'I will be with you somewhat towards the end of May,' he wrote Mareste, in rather better English than most of his infrequent attempts: 'the hunger brings the wolf out of the forest.' But in May he was still in Milan.

His safety there was now threatened. The police and the Austrian authorities were taking rough measures against liberals, and even as a foreigner he was not safe from arrest. His mind made up, he went for ten days to his beloved Lake Como, and the day after he came back had a last meeting with Métilde. It was the tearing out of a nerve, and he left Milan in an agony of mind and spirit in which his only coherent thought was that no one must be allowed to see that he was unhappy, still madly in love, suffering, for a woman he had never had—*ne pas être deviné*—his deepest impulse.

Henri Beyle possessed a degree of the caution and reticence, the aggressive determination not to be taken in or ridiculed, of his hard Dauphinois stock: it played a natural enough part in his reluctance to trust even close friends. More to be regretted is the effect on a very vulnerable and passionate child of learning to protect his acute need of affection from being scared by incomprehension or mockery. That was irreparable. Irreparable so far as his personal life was concerned. Triumphantly overcome in solitude by the writer of his two great novels. In personal life he opened himself to very few—to one or two women with whom he was not in love, and to perhaps only one man, significantly not a Frenchman. He met the Neapolitan exile Domenico di Fiore in Paris soon after he went back; and very slowly, over years, learned that he could trust him. It is of di Fiore that he thinks when he begins the *Vie de Henry Brulard*. To whom else could he have written, two years before his death: '. . . au total, vaut-il la peine de vivre?'

Chapter 7

HE HAD COME back with the idea of getting himself a government place. It foundered on his instinctive reluctance. It was another seven years before he began seriously to solicit—a word he pronounced with loathing.

He slipped back easily into the mould of a way of life laid up in his mind even before he came to Paris for the first time and instead of settling down sensibly to the École Polytechnique began, until he fell into Daru hands, to prepare himself to be the new Molière. He returned to it eagerly when he had got himself out of uniform in 1802, and again when his career as auditor came to its abrupt end. And again now, in 1821. Writing, serious reading, friends, music, salons, a café—his basic needs.

He met Mérimée for the first time not long after his return, the beginning of a friendship as close and important to him as any in his life, unaffected by the difference in age—he was twenty years the elder—yet carrying the seeds of estrangement. They were so closely linked, so similar in tastes and habits, that their unlikeness sharpens the image of Beyle himself. They are most alike in a quivering hypersensitivity and in the care both took to hide it, even from each other. So far as we know, only once in a matter touching his deepest most secret emotions did Beyle talk to Mérimée with complete confidence in his affection and understanding, and even then he was not honest by the letter. No more than Beyle was Mérimée willing to give himself away; and what one of his biographers calls his 'fausse impassibilité' hid a capacity for suffering, and griefs, one in particular, as deep as anything Beyle endured, and ineffaceable. Even when they seem most alike there is more than a touch of unlikeness. There are passages of the grossest indecency in Beyle's intimate journals, letters, conversation, but they have not the frightening obscenity of some of Mérimée's letters, and not the cruelty of some of his comments on women, which startle when one remembers the exquisite delicacy of his relations with women he respected and loved: there is something frenzied in the debauchery he plunged into during a rather short period of years, a curiously cold bawdiness, an icy *nostalgie de la boue*, at the opposite pole from the dryness of his comments on what he regarded as offensive passages in *Le Rouge et le Noir*. In Henri Beyle there remains, even at his coarsest, most graceless, a flicker of the innocence of the seventeen-year-old setting off to Italy, mad with joy, on his way to a commission in the Sixth Dragoons. 'Avec toutes celles-là'—a man of fifty-two is scrawling in the dust on the edge of an Italian lake the initials of the women he has loved—'et avec plusieurs autres, j'ai toujours été un enfant; aussi ai-je eu très peu de succès'. Where his over-sensitive heart was engaged he was the least accomplished of seducers.

One of Mérimée's most attractive qualities—he had many—was the tenderness of his attachment to a few men, a warmth of concern and love I am rather certain he never felt for Henri Beyle. There is nothing in the story of Beyle's friendships like Mérimée's anguished grief for the painful death at thirty-one of their common friend Victor Jacquemont. All his life Beyle was more loosely attached to his male friends, however intimate. Where he and Mérimée differ completely is in their attitude—speaking roughly—to getting on. Even in his furiously dissipated youth Mérimée never ceased to pursue his career wisely and steadily. Already in his late twenties he was a successful author, with the right friends, men like Sainte-Beuve and Victor Hugo; he impressed important people not only by his talents, but by the steadiness below the whoring and the cynical wit. He was a serious scholar, an excellent linguist—Greek, Latin, English, Spanish, German, and later Russian—and a staunch and indefatigable fighter against vandalism on every level, clerical, military, political. He moved easily and naturally in official and aristocratic circles. He had none of Beyle's restlessness, passionate enthusiasms, blindness to the consequences of a decision or a choice.

Pointless to weigh the human value of the *Chartreuse de Parme* against the magnificent heritage which the younger writer's years of service as Inspector of Historic Monuments left to the civilised world. The two men served different demons.

During these first months in Paris, Beyle was profoundly bored and unsettled. He was racked by his longing for Métilde, and racked in a different way by the loss of his manuscript. His days fell into a pattern which was a mocking reflection of his life in Milan: he rose late, took his coffee and two brioches at the café de Rouen with Mareste and his cousin Romain Colomb, 'mon ami Colomb, qui braverait les supplices pour sa parole et pour moi', devoted to him since their schooldays in Grenoble; walked with Mareste as far as his office in the *Préfecture de Police*; sauntered along the quais, and read Shakespeare under the leafy chestnuts of the Tuileries, his attention wandering from the page to a dream of Métilde. At five he went back to the hotel for M. Petit's admirable table d'hôte. In the evening a café, a salon. With her old kindness, Mme Beugnot had opened her house to him again as soon as he returned. And there were others.

In October he went to London, his second visit, with Mareste and another man, staying at the Tavistock Hotel in Covent Garden: he visited museums, theatres, and the ball at Almack's, and walked about Chelsea: he was enchanted by the Thames at Richmond and quietly happy with a very small gently appealing young prostitute living in decent poverty in south London. Although he considered the English to be the most obtuse and barbarous nation in the world London soothed him, and when his friends left he stayed on, until the end of November, six weeks.

He was down to his last franc when he went back to Paris, willing to take anything, any position—an almost infallible recipe for not getting one. But very shortly after his return the missing manuscript of *De l'amour* turned up. His relief was overwhelming. He set to work at once, revising, adding to it, demanding contributions from his friends. One of these, a hard-drinking character named Edward Edwards, found him a publisher willing to produce the book at his own charge, and in the following summer Beyle had the proofs in his hands. He rented a room in the village of Montmorency, two hours by coach from Paris, and worked on them in solitude, torturing himself with thoughts of Métilde and Milan. In the end he fled to Mme Beugnot's country house at Bonneuil-sur-Marne and finished his corrections there, less wretchedly, since after working all day in the grounds of the chateau he could spend the evening in the drawing-room. Here with a twinge of interest he caught the glance Mme Beugnot's young married daughter, the Comtesse Curial, fixed on him. He was too sunk in the past to read the signal his future was sending him.

De l'amour came out in August. It was a failure. So crushing a failure that two years later, on 3 April 1824, the publisher, F. Mongie, was writing: 'Je désirerais bien être arrivé au moment où je devrais vous faire compte des bénéfices que j'espérais avoir sur votre ouvrage *De l'amour*, mais je commence à croire que cette époque n'arrivera pas, je n'ai pas vendu quarante exemplaires de ce livre. . . .'

The failure of this one of his books grieved and vexed him. In another part of the literary wood his situation improved: this year he began to write articles for the newly started *Paris Monthly Review*, an English magazine published in Paris, and in the *New Monthly Magazine*, one of several magazines owned by Colburn. He had had to do with Colburn about the London editions of *Rome, Naples et Florence*, but in this instance he seems to have been helped by an Irishman living in Paris, called Bartholemew Stritch, whom he describes as impassive, melancholy and strictly honest. During the next six or seven years he worked for Colburn regularly, sending him lively informative essays on French literature, politics, manners. He was the most professional of writers; he worked solidly until five in the evening, and when he stopped shut his mind to it and became the other, the social Beyle. Dressed with a dandified care, he paid a visit to one or other of the houses where he was welcome, or to the opera, or he dined with friends, in a good restaurant. He was happiest of all in a politely amusing salon—'Un salon de huit ou dix personnes dont toutes les femmes ont eu des amants, où la conversation est gaie, anecdotique, et où l'on prend un punch léger à minuit et demi, est l'endroit du monde où je me trouve le mieux. . . .' (*Brulard*) When he wrote that he was in Civitavecchia, where witty intelligent talk was hard to come by. Ah, poor Beyle.

His most important salon, that of the Comte de Tracy, in the rue d'Anjou, was not of this celestial kind. In *Souvenirs d'Égotisme* he draws a superb full-length portrait of the great philosopher, 60, well-built, invariably wearing black, standing in front of his fireplace talking with an exquisite politeness to academicians, ex-ambassadors, ministers, scholars, writers, all the great or about to be great figures of the Restoration years, the historian Thierry, Benjamin Constant, Général de Lafayette, tall, bent, impassive, and still at the age of seventy-five with an eye for a shapely young breast. To be an habitué of this salon opened to him other houses which might be useful to him. If after a visit they bored him, he rarely went again: unlike his friend Mérimée he was almost involuntarily given to ignoring chances to advance himself. 'J'ai vécu dix ans dans ce salon,' he remarks, 'reçu poliment, estimé, mais tous les jours moins *lié*, excepté avec mes amis. C'est là un des défauts de mon caractère. C'est ce défaut qui fait que je ne m'en prends pas aux hommes de mon peu d'avancement.'

He was, so he says, intimidated by the number of people it was obligatory to greet as soon as you came in: the Tracy family was enormous, three generations, down to a row of fifteen or twenty young grand-daughters and their suitors. If he was intimidated, which one doubts, he clung the more readily to the two members of the family who approved of him, Mme de Tracy herself, with her constant gentle kindness for him, and her English daughter-in-law, the wife of Victor de Tracy, spirited, elegant, to Beyle's mind a little too thin but very charming. She may at the time have been a little in love with him, she was certainly a loyal friend when, after the 1830 revolution, he was forced to solicit in earnest.

He was not wholly a success in the aristocratic Tracy salon. His irreverent wit and not seldom violently indiscreet opinions displeased some of his listeners, among them at times his host. How many incorrigible mockers at hypocrisy, obsequious conformism, self-regarding prudence, can society stand? That his derisively cynical conversation and indifference to the offence it might give was a mask—not to be mocked he mocked—is a half-truth. The other half of the truth is that to be in knowledgeable company, prepared even if disapproving him to listen and argue, intoxicated him and he talked with a reckless gaiety, exaggerating ferociously opinions he sincerely held or had held in his Jacobin childhood: he was enjoying himself. He was many men, and one of them was gaily excitable, friendly, impulsive, and carelessly indiscreet.

One person sensitive enough to know this was Mérimée. 'Il était très gai dans le monde,' he noted in his *H.B.*, 'fou quelquefois, négligeant trop les convenances et les susceptibilités. Souvent il était de mauvais ton, mais toujours spirituel et original.' One sees Mérimée listening, half alarmed for his friend, half maliciously watching him overdo his audacity and needlessly offend people it would be wiser not to offend.

He made another close friend here in Victor Jacquemont, explorer and naturalist, a friend of Mérimée's, and like Mérimée much younger than he was, eighteen years younger. Tall, slender, well-bred, with a natural charm, he pleased Beyle enormously. They met as equals; Henri Beyle was devoid of any feeling that he ought to be treated with respect by younger men: none of his friends felt they need handle him carefully, and Victor Jacquemont wrote to him about his work as to an intimate of his own age, with a brutal candour the older man accepted with calm indifference. Mérimée again, in the same memoir: 'Je n'ai connu personne qui fût plus galant homme à recevoir les critiques sur ses ouvrages. Ses amis lui parlaient toujours sans le moindre ménagement.' It was not that he was thick-skinned. On the contrary. No writer ever had a thinner skin. 'Il me semble,' he wrote in his pamphlet on Racine and Shakespeare, 'qu'il faut du courage à l'écrivain presque autant qu'au guerrier; l'un ne doit pas plus songer aux journalistes que l'autre à l'hôpital.' The truth is that he

95

was mortally certain that if he showed he had been stung he would be laughed at, to his face or behind his back. This is pudor, not vanity: he was nearly as devoid of vanity as of envy. And he had few illusions about himself, even as a writer. His stoical acceptance of critical abuse was a habit learned so young that it had become second nature, a nearly involuntary reflex of his mind: the pain of the sting did not last longer than a few minutes. In a rather dry way, too, he was able to look at himself as writer without first putting the mirror in a kind light: a virtue rare even in the finer sort of writer. And he could give as good as he got.

He was something of a failure again in the fashionable salon to which he was taken by the critic and historian Claude Fauriel, a friend for whom he had an unusual respect, writing of him as 'a man of the highest merit, not a charlatan'. His hostess, Mlle Mary Clarke, was a little shrewish Irishwoman, slightly deformed, who had been living in France since 1814. Again he talked too much and too well, alienating her by his seemingly heartless theories: after a year or two she quarrelled with him, and, to his annoyance, Fauriel, her permanent and permanently bachelor lover—he appears as an incongruously Shavian character in this modish circle—took her part.

He was more at his ease though no less imprudent in salons where the discussion remained on a serious literary and philo-sophical level. In the house shared by Viollet-le-Duc and his brother-in-law Étienne Delécluze he was able to spend Friday evening in the superb library of the former and Sunday afternoon in the small fifth-floor apartment where the circumspect and intellectually stolid art critic of the *Journal des Débats* received a small number of friends, for the most part younger liberal writers and journalists. Sainte-Beuve, who was amused by Beyle, says he helped himself freely to news and ideas he used in the articles he was sending to his London journals: no doubt he did, and no doubt Delécluze, with his own critical column to fill, was not altogether pleased: his opinion of his liveliest guest was ambi-valent; he was penetrating enough to appreciate his guest's rare distinction but, good bourgeois that he was, he could not stomach

Beyle's mockery of personages he thought over-praised or who bored him. One of Beyle's gibes stuck quivering in his mind for years. Beyle recorded it himself in *Brulard*. 'Bossuet . . . c'est de la blague sérieuse.' Easy enough, glancing round the literary market at this or any moment, to recognise the animal, but the epithet itself is untranslatable. Writing twenty years after Beyle died, Delécluze recalled it slightly differently. But he recalled it.

Whatever else Beyle did with his evening he tried to end it in the hôtel de Lillois in the drawing-room of the young and famous Italian singer, Mme Pasta. He had heard her in Milan. She received from eleven o'clock: he rarely left, and then with reluctance, before three. He met his more intimate friends here, Mérimée, Victor Jacquemont, Mareste, who had brought him here in the first place, Jean-Alexandre Buchon, and that friend with whom at every meeting he felt safer, Domenico di Fiore. What above all he found in this salon was contentment, of a rare kind. He could be silent here: Madame Pasta spoke Milanese to him, and there were always Italian visitors with whom he could talk of Milan. He could not make himself ask about Métilde, but now and then someone would speak her name, stopping his heart for a moment.

Some time in the spring of 1822 he moved, with the proofs of *De l'amour* in his baggage, to a room on the second and later one on the third floor of the hôtel de Lillois. He says that this move and his friendship with the singer damaged him in M. de Tracy's eyes. It had more than one benefit. His room was next door to the one occupied by Mme Pasta's singing-master, accompanist, secretary, what you will, a young Belgian called Michereux, with whom he could talk usefully about music: in Milan he had heard and discussed their work with modern composers, including the young Rossini, now beginning to be much talked of in Paris and London. He was more critical of Rossini's operas than when he heard the earlier ones at the Scala—not that even then he had placed him with Cimarosa and Mozart. But he knew more about him than anyone else in France and he seized the chance. The article he wrote on him in the *Paris Monthly Review* was plagiarised in

London—he, of all writers, could not complain—and he developed it into a book, *Memoirs of Rossini by the author of the Life of Haydn and Mozart*, for an English publisher, and while it was slowly being translated prepared a much fuller and better work which came out in Paris in November 1823, three months ahead of the English version. It was not a complete biography, nor did it deal with the later operas, but it was informative, lively, witty, and appearing almost as Rossini arrived in Paris it sold honourably well.

He had less success with a short and more important work. On 31 July and 2 August a company of English actors attempting to bring Shakespeare to the heathen were hissed off the stage at the Théâtre de la Porte-Saint-Martin by patriotic characters shouting: 'Down with Shakespeare! He's one of Wellington's men!' Beyle's indignant article entitled—let me keep his spelling—*Racine et Shakspeare* in the October *Paris Monthly Review* was not simply a piece of adroitly timed journalism. It sprang from his mature judgement. He had been seduced by Shakespeare as a thirteen-year-old schoolboy, had read him in Italy in 1800, in his garret in the rue d'Angivillier ('Je passe sans cesse pour ce grand homme du plus tendre amour à la plus vive admiration. . . . C'est pour mon cœur le plus grand poète qui ait existé . . .'), in Marseille, in Germany, and in Paris during years of opulence, when he bought himself a superb edition in thirty volumes. His article became the first chapter of a fifty-five-page pamphlet. It came out in March 1823, almost unnoticed except by fellow critics. But the argument was a live one; and two years later the second and longer edition established him, for the first time solidly, in literary circles in Paris—but in literary circles books are acquired, not bought, and there was no sale.

Romanticism was in the air in France as in Italy. In Milan, in Msgr de Brême's salon, he had argued furiously for Shakespeare against Racine, with as much delight in shocking his hearers as in bruiting his own verities. But he was not a dadaist, not an iconoclast gaily knocking the heads off old images: he was deeply serious. His demands were sober: abolish the unities, no restriction on the action of a play, tragedies in prose, not 'l'abominable chant du vers alexandrin'. There may be something of the fox without a tail in all revolutionaries: he had never mastered the alexandrine, never succeeded in writing tolerable verse. In its broadest sense he explained romanticism in literature as the expression of a living sensibility, addressed to contemporaries. If a Phèdre, then a Phèdre breathing the emotional and moral atmosphere and confronting the complexities of her own time. His romanticism is *sui generis*—'Peut-être,' he said in *Racine et Shakspeare*, 'faut-il être *romantique* dans les idées: le siècle le veut ainsi; mais soyons *classiques* dans les expressions'. So, by instinct and in practice he is: the men and women of his novels are passionate extremists, outrageously individual; the language in which he lays them open, exposing nerves and heart, is deliciously clear, subtle in implication, ruthlessly truthful in its analyses of emotion—and lucid. Descriptions of places and objects are brief: night in the Verrières garden, and the emotion felt by Julien and Mme de Rênal, are evoked by the wind swaying through the branches of the lime and the fall of a few drops of rain on the leaves. His narrative is dense, woven closely of the experiences, memories, reflections, reveries, of his whole life. Hence the intensity, the plenitude, of novels written with surprising speed by a man who with hard effort had learned to know himself as coolly as no other novelist has done, not even that great auto-vivisectionist, Marcel Proust.

He had no liking for the great romantics of his day—'Les romantiques sont les gens les plus sec et les plus plats du monde, de vrai fats littéraires.' He detested Chateaubriand—'hypocrite le plus consommé de France'—almost every phrase of his careful prose false in sentiment and reasoning alike. If he had lived to read the *Mémoires* would he have forgiven him *Atala* and the rest? I believe so. He could not forgive Mme de Stael her abominable pretence of emotions she was incapable of feeling. He cared little for Vigny, and for Victor Hugo less, a disdain the other returned heartily. His only known comment on *Hernani*—he attended the première—is briefly dismissive. Sainte-Beuve, who was present at an encounter when Mérimée brought the two together, reported that they were like two wild cats from opposite gutters, fur bristling and claws gingerly drawn in.

From November 1823 to March he spent four and a half months in Italy, two of them in Rome, where Delécluze and others of his friends were staying. Delécluze found him an easier companion here, less unmanageably provocative, and very gay, a fountain of energy and gaiety. It may have been that Delécluze was learning to attend more calmly to Beyle's unorthodox views. But Beyle in Italy was contented and less ironically on his guard than in any other place.

His life was changing. Back in Paris, he added to the several journals, English and French, with which he collaborated regularly, the *Journal de Paris*, writing for it on art and music: to get it was a stroke of luck he owed to Mareste and another friend. During these years between 1823 and 1827 his income rose from the penury of the months after Milan to between nine and ten thousand francs, some three-quarters of it earned. His new ease allowed him to dress with a careful elegance which he thought turned attention away from his ugliness. Was he ugly? He believed so. Yet from descriptions left of him, and one or two portraits, one sees very clearly why in spite of his increasing corpulence he charmed. The fine lines of the mouth, the light half-sceptical half-tender smile, are infinitely attractive. Eyes and mouth are the features in a man which appeal most strongly to women, and in Beyle did—except to Mme Dembowski.

Métilde had become a memory, one of those memories, happily rare, able at moments to thrust a claw from its cerements. Abruptly this year he gave himself up soul and body to the second serious passion of his life—if you care to count the Pietragrua, the third. Since his passing view of her in her mother's chateau he had thought now and again about Clémentine Curial—in his private language, Menti—and it was, he says, timidity, the consciousness of his ugliness, which kept him from falling in love with her. Perhaps. Perhaps if he had not been spending the entire day obsessed with thoughts of Métilde he might have risked a rebuff. She remained in his mind: he had even visited her in her chateau near Compiègne during one of General Curial's absences in the army. She became his mistress a year later, soon after he returned from the visit to Rome. She was thirty-five at the time and he forty-one. It was a violent encounter between two passionate highly-strung and on Menti's part ungovernable temperaments. She was charming to look at, frank, lively, sensual, and she had the wit to appreciate his originality and even at moments to find him touchingly vulnerable. She was capable of tenderness and of quite appalling fits of rage, but not of constancy—and how one prefers her to the cultivated well-behaved Métilde.

By the spring of 1826 the storm was wearing out in her. He had —of course he had—a strategy for handling the situation, and the fatuity to think it would succeed with a clever highly-bred woman: in June he went to London, to give her time to miss him.

Again he stayed in Covent Garden, this time at Hummums Hotel—a letter he wrote to his friend Sutton Sharpe in February 1827 was signed Old Hummums. He spent a great part of the twelve weeks he was in England with this friend, a rapidly rising young barrister he had met for the first time four years earlier: immensely talented, judicious, liberal in politics, cultivated, pleasure-loving, he charmed Beyle as he charmed most people. Fourteen years younger than Beyle, he belonged to that breed of Englishmen for whom France is a country of the heart. He was in France whenever he could contrive it; his intimate friends were French, Mérimée, Beyle, Buchon, Victor Jacquemont, Mareste; his ties with them were strong and brotherly, he shared their social life and their dissipations, introduced them in London society, entertained them at the Athenæum, cheerfully undertook endless errands and commissions for them in London. During this visit Beyle went with him to the assizes in Lancaster, travelled in the north of the country, visited the lakes, and stayed in country houses where he was pleased by the kindness of his hosts and mildly shocked to notice that women were treated as inferior human beings: 'Leur grand vertu est le dévouement, vertu des esclaves. . . .' He was writing to Madame Jules Gaulthier, his *amiable et bonne Jules*: perhaps he exaggerated a little to amuse her. In September a letter from Menti violently disquieted him. He left London at once, travelling with Sutton Sharpe, and reached Paris to find he had been displaced by a younger man, her husband's aide-de-camp. He felt his dismissal acutely. The pain will have been adulterated by hurt vanity; he had had her and had failed to keep her. But it went deep. Speaking about her ten years later he astounded Mérimée by the only tears his friend ever saw him shed. The incident is recorded in *H.B.* They had met, after a long separation, in the little town of Laon, on the 4th of August 1836. They spent the evening walking up and down, up and down, under the trees of the deserted promenade, talking. An intolerable pressure of grief drove Beyle to confide in his friend that a woman who had been his mistress for a long time, many years, was breaking with him, unable, she had told him, to believe that at her age he still loved her.

He was not telling Mérimée the truth, but neither was he precisely lying. The truth was that he had seen Menti at this time, ten years after the break, had fallen in love with her again and was begging her to take him back. I daresay without hope. The impulse to comfort himself by talking about it to this close friend was stronger than his reticence. But he did not drop the mask completely: it was easier, less humiliating, to speak as though an affair which had been going on unbroken for twelve years was only now ending. As in a bitter sense it was. Moreover, it is certain, as certain as anything one knows about the human heart is certain, that a deeper colder river ran below the torrent of regret for Menti: a memory of his unmitigated failure with that Mètilde 'who would not tell me she loved me'.

Menti refused him. It was very sensible of her. She was gentle with him. Yet when she said, 'How can you still love me? I am forty-five?' what she meant was—surely?—'How can you expect me to take in my arms a man of fifty-three, corpulent almost to deformity?' But their friendship and a kindness for him persisted in her, together with the egotistical certainty that he must want to help her. To the end of her life—she died, unmourned, Mme Jules Gaulthier told him, by her unkind children, two years before he did—she turned to him for advice as she might have turned to an indulgent brother.

It was a long time, months, after his hurried return from England before Beyle lost his arid sense of humiliation. He sunk himself in work. He took up again a novel he had started in January but had abandoned almost at once, and completed it in three weeks between September and October. The origins of *Armance* are not important, and its unstated theme, sexual impotence—dwelt on at length in the cynically indecent letter he wrote Mérimée in December—is nearly irrelevant. The impulse that turned a faulty ill-constructed novel into an elegiac story of an impossible love affair is his own bitter experience of failure. The ripple of mocking wit and the satiric portrait of aristocratic Parisian society sets a sharp edge on the young lovers' fragile happiness, reveries, and ethereal sadness. Let me quote Gide— from a preface written in 1925: 'J'aurais dû dire encore que, de tout les livres de Stendhal, je tiens celui-ci pour le plus délicat et le plus joliment écrit. . . .'

He had been a child when he decided that all he wanted in life was to write like Molière. He was an ex-soldier of nineteen when he shut himself in his attic in the rue d'Angivillier to prepare for his future greatness. He is now forty-three: it has taken him twenty-four years to admit that his strenuously cultivated powers of psychological analysis are useless in the theatre and that the novel is the place for them. He has sixteen years left.

Possibly his unhappiness, hidden from friends he met in society, opened him to friendship with two charming and very civilised women, alike only in the sincerity of an affection for him which offered the most vulnerable, most self-critical of men what he deeply needed, a sense of security. Both these women wrote marvellous letters, witty, thoughtful, sensible, without a trace of the self-awareness which is the original sin of very intelligent women, altogether enchanting letters. He had met Jules Gaulthier already, when she was young Jules de la Bergerie, trying to comfort

the stricken Crozet in his unattractive despair. When she married
M. Gaulthier, a tax official, four years later, Beyle lost sight of her.
Now, early in this fatal year of 1826 he met her again, living with
her husband on the outskirts of Paris. The letter he wrote her from
London in September, half mockingly affectionate, is one any
self-possessed woman would read with amused liking for the
writer, and a tremor of reserve: had she been less poised, a
friendship he came to rely on would not have lasted him to his
death.

Sophie Duvaucel was the step-daughter, by her mother's second
marriage—her first husband was guillotined during the Revolution—of the naturalist Georges Cuvier, to whose highly regarded
Saturday evening receptions in his house at the Jardin des Plantes
Beyle was taken by Buchon. An odd character, Cuvier. For all his
eminence—in the judgement of Sir Alister Hardy in his 1963–4
Gifford Lectures, he was 'perhaps the greatest of comparative
anatomists . . . who from his position in Paris dominated European
zoology for so long'—he was notoriously obsequious. 'Quelle n'a
pas été la servilité et la bassesse envers le pouvoir de M. Cuvier,'
Beyle says of him in *Brulard*. But he was genial enough to let
Beyle try to argue with him. Sophie—Mlle Sophie, Beyle called
her—was a delicately seductive young woman, warm-hearted,
direct, probably the wittiest and most intelligent of all the women
Beyle knew. He had too much respect for her step-father's genius,
and for her fineness and breeding, to fall in love with her: oddly,
he seems to have had for her something of the liking, without the
gross freedom in argument, that he might feel for a charming
intelligent young man, a Victor Jacquemont: the 'Écrivez-moi,
mon ami tout court,' in a letter he wrote her from Civitavecchia
in November 1834 is the measure of his comradely ease with her,
and but for her unshakeable and clearsighted regard for him he
might not have lasted long enough in the abstruse air of this salon
to become, as he did, a family friend. He introduced Mérimée to
the family, not entirely to Mérimée's acute sense of fitness.
'Après tout, Mlle Sophie est toujours très aimable,' he confided to
Sutton Sharpe in January 1829, 'mais je regrette beaucoup d'avoir

été presenté dans cette maison par Beyle car il m'a chargé de sa mauvaise réputation et j'ai bien assez de mienne.'

It was probably Beyle who presented the Englishman to Sophie. This is not the place to follow the traces of a passion which after two years of hope and disappointment was defeated by Sophie's reluctance to leave a step-father desperately dependent on her help in his work and a mother broken by the death of the last remaining of her children by Cuvier, and defeated finally by a lover drily tired of the long drawn-out effort. The story is one Stendhal should have written.

Early in 1827 he sent a finally revised manuscript of *Armance* to its publisher, Urbain Canel, who was paying him a thousand francs for the right to publish. Its success—he expected it to succeed— was acutely important to him. Abruptly, in February, his London editor had cancelled his contract, cutting off at a stroke two-thirds of his income, and four months later his most profitable French source dried up when the *Journal de Paris* folded. From what had been, for him, affluence, he was plunged into poverty again. Neither his violent protests nor the efforts on his behalf of Sutton Sharpe and the honest melancholy Stritch wrung from Colburn anything except promises, not kept.

He behaved in this crisis exactly as, knowing him, one would expect. A familiar urgency to get away seized him and as soon as he had corrected the proofs of his novel, without waiting for it to come out, he went off to Italy.

He lived abroad for a good six months. From Genoa, where he was made splendidly welcome, he sailed to Naples, and craving solitude went to Ischia—'J'ai passé dix jours en pension chez un paysan . . . c'est délicieux,' he told Mareste. He spent four weeks in Naples, and nearly as long in Rome. Then Florence. Here he stayed for more than two months, enchanted by the theatre, the splendid balls, the dinner-parties, the pretty Englishwomen, all of them, he told Mareste, 'bête comme des pots'. An anything but stupid young Frenchwoman, Hortense Allart, was in Florence at this moment, passing through an early stage of her spirited career; she had two confessional novels under her arm, and she honeyed Beyle into a promise to find a publisher for one of them, a promise he kept; but by the time the book came out she was in Rome, preparing to sink her delicate claws into the ageing Chateaubriand.

Probably the most subtle pleasure he had here, and the one that kept him contented so long, was his conversations with Lamartine, here as first secretary in the embassy. They had met already in Paris, in Mme Mareste's salon. Thirty-seven years later, in his *Cours*, Lamartine recorded their talk, no doubt with a certain heightening.

When, towards the end of the year, Beyle left Florence, he must have been nearing the end of his resources. Even had the police not thrown him out of Milan at twelve hours' notice—he spent his one evening at the Scala—he could hardly have afforded to stay there, and Paris, when he arrived on 28 January 1828, offered only problems. *Armance*, treated as coldly by his friends as by the few reviewers who touched it—'n'annonçait nulle invention et nul génie' (Sainte-Beuve)—had been as near as no matter a complete failure. His money troubles worsened. The War Office was proposing to axe his small pension, and he began the weary recital of his claims in a long letter of 3 July 1828 to Général Décaux, Minister of War—'Monseigneur, J'ai l'honneur de mettre sous les yeux de Votre Excellence ma cessation de payement du 30 Juin 1828 . . . j'ai passé le grand Saint-Bernard avec le premier consul Bonaparte . . . j'ai servé comme adjoint aux commissaires des guerres la veille de la bataille d'Iéna. . . . J'ai fait les campagnes de 1806, 1807, et 1808' . . . and the rest of it and the rest of it. In the end he was allowed to keep half—four hundred and fifty francs— reducing his only assured income, with the annuity, to some two thousand francs.

He did not need to be told that he must try for a government place. He knew it.

Advised and encouraged by Mareste, he tried unsuccessfully for a place in the Royal Archives; it would have given him a salary of one thousand seven hundred francs and an apartment in the hôtel de Soubise. He turned for help to Apollinaire d'Argout and to another of his distinguished former colleagues on the Conseil d'État, the Comte Amédée de Pastoret, and—this must have given him a wry twinge—to Édouard Mounier, now Baron Mounier, approaching him with formal respect. Supported with unfailing loyalty by Pastoret, by Cuvier acting at the promptings of his step-daughter, by Mounier, and with characteristic energy by Pierre Daru, he nevertheless failed to get a subordinate post as librarian in the Bibliothèque Royal. Why, with such backing, the failures? Doubts that he could be relied on to curb his levity and lack of reverence for powerful bores? Or had some of his backers mental reserves—certainly not Pastoret, and not, probably, Daru with his strong sense of family obligation.

Only to *need* help desperately at the age of forty-six is an indiscretion.

The years of 1828 and 1829 were a very low point in his life. It is one thing to be poor and insecure as a young man, a hind let loose, and quite another to be soliciting in late middle age. He became profoundly discouraged and, if one believes him, thought of shooting himself. I doubt it. I doubt entirely that for all his habit, or vice, of day-dreaming, and his nervous susceptibility, he was ever in danger of suicide, in his despair now or after Clémentine threw him over or during the years when he was obsessed by his anguished memories of Métilde. Sprung from hard stock, his life from earliest adolescence was a blundering but resolute progress to self-discipline. The writer of the youthful letters to Pauline with their insistence that happiness is the rigorous study of oneself and others—'connaître à fond les hommes'—trained himself in lucidity, in self-criticism, in the art of existing, as he might have trained for the diplomatic service or to play the cello supremely well: he matured and suffered, without for a vital minute losing sight of his aim. His obstinacy, his reasoned and passionate will to live as he chose, put it beyond belief that in the circumstances of his life as we know it he would have admitted defeat. The impulse to ignore failure, to go on, to go on, to the last given minute, was involuntary.

Ludicrous to suppose that he gave a great deal of time to sombre reflection on his downfall. During these straitened years he can hardly have spent an evening alone. If he had not as yet any very secure standing as a writer, he was securely established and at ease in the most distinguished literary salons of the time, meeting the same brilliant company, the same friends, men and women, throughout the week: '. . . le mardi chez Madame Ancelot, le mercredi chez Gérard, le samedi chez M. Cuvier, trois soupers par semaine au Café Anglais, et je suis au courant de ce qui se dit à Paris,' he told di Fiore in the nostalgic letter he sent him from Civitavecchia on 1 November 1834. The regular members of the small group of male friends who dined together two or three times a week at the Café Anglais or the Frères provençaux included Mérimée, Mareste, Beyle, Eugène Delacroix, Victor Jacquemont, Alfred de Musset, and whenever he was in Paris Sutton Sharpe, evenings which sometimes, after hours of drinking and of intelligent indiscreet talk, ended in a brothel. It was the period of Beyle's closest intimacy with Mérimée, before his own absence from Paris and Mérimée's growing official importance made a little plain what might otherwise not have become plain, that at a depth they were incompatible, dissonant.

The aristocratic salon in the rue d'Anjou was open to him still, and if a cold flicker of disapproval of his more ironic and destructive comments was apparent in his host's glances, the warmth of his daughter-in-law's welcome hid it: Madame Victor de Tracy had a concern for Henri Beyle, and during the next months showed it.

I am sure of one thing: he was not bored. The shifts he was put to in keeping up appearances with his well-placed friends were more tolerable than, later, the boredom of his consulate where, as in the same letter he told di Fiore: 'Je crève d'ennui; je ne puis faire la conversation avec personne. . . .' He had a pleasant third-floor room in the hôtel de Valois, 71 rue de Richelieu—in exile he recalled it with nostalgic regret. And whatever his thoughts when, alone after a brilliant evening, he removed his wig, glanced down at a too prominent stomach, and prepared himself to sleep, they were surely not of suicide.

He was working, and in July he showed his cousin Romain Colomb the unfinished manuscript of a book on Rome. Colomb not only gave him sensible advice—to make it a complete portrait of Rome, ancient and modern—but offered to help him with the research. *Promenades dans Rome* became an incomparably lively blend of history, the arts, the monuments, music, politics, the social scene, and its author's vividly imagined adventures and companions. A visitor to Rome today will do very well to carry it in his baggage, without troubling himself overmuch about errors of detail and without requiring that everything Beyle related of his own activities should be truer than the truest of fictions. Published the following year (1829) in September, it brought him a much needed one thousand five hundred francs. It was praised, too, in the right quarters.

Once it was off his hands he decided that he needed to travel, and he arranged to leave for Bordeaux on the evening of 8 September. That morning, reading the newspapers over his coffee and brioches in the café de Rouen, he came on the anouncement of Pierre Daru's death. It shocked him. Since his return to France he had neglected the Darus. Partly, no doubt, because, Alexandrine dead, their drawing-room was dull and stiffly formal, but surely, too, because it was the one place where neither eloquence nor wit would hide the fact that in Daru eyes he had made a failure of his life.

Seized by remorse for his graceless behaviour, he rushed to the once familiar house in the rue de Grenelle. He was admitted by a footman in tears, and wept with him. Not, I think, for the disappearance of his savage benefactor. For the colder change in his own life.

He had no impulse to put his journey off for three days to attend the funeral. From Bordeaux he went to Perpignan and crossed into Spain—no farther than Barcelona: the shortness of his stay suggests that he was as unacceptable to authority here as he had been in Milan. Then Grenoble—after ten years. He took the trouble to go out to his father's estate at Claix, now sold. Walking the five or six miles as a rebellious child did? Then—some time in

October—Marseille. Was he actively groping into the past? He may well have been: the pleasure he took in reliving and re-arranging his past persisted to the end of his life.

What actually he found in Marseille was not his infatuated younger self but his arguably immortal future.

Chapter 8

THE SOURCE OF *Le Rouge et le Noir* in a murder committed two years before this, in the country near Grenoble, is of minor interest. Who knows why a fragment of overheard dialogue or an item of news read by chance suddenly releases a novelist's deepest emotions and powers, at the time, or days or years later. Some stirring in Henri Beyle's mind during the night of 25/26 October engendered there the idea of turning a violent episode into a novel. He began to draft it the next morning and worked with feverish energy for rather longer than four weeks. He was quite capable of covering in that time two or three hundred pages with his terrible writing, so that what he had in his baggage when he went back to Paris on December 3 was at the very least the emergent contours of a great novel, greater than anything he had yet attempted.

He did not immediately look at the manuscript again. During his absence an affair (to call it an affair of the heart would be to misplace it), begun earlier in the year when Eugène Delacroix took him and Mareste to call on a cousin, currently his mistress, had fallen apart. Alberthe de Rubempré was young, attractive, free-spoken, witty, a demi-intellectual. She provoked Beyle to a sensual frenzy. In June, with or without Delacroix's knowledge, she became his mistress. Perhaps with. After a first cold impression when he met Beyle at one of Gérard's Wednesdays, he had come to feel something like a concern for the man he speaks about in his *Journal* with half-pitying warmth. For Delacroix he is still, eleven years after his death, 'le pauvre Beyle' . . . 'Où est le pauvre Beyle? . . .' No one else speaks of him so. The echo of Villon, doubtless unconscious, moves me.

As 'le pauvre Beyle' should have expected of Alberthe, but did not, he had been supplanted. By, of all people, Mareste. It was a mortifying experience, an unforgivable stroke from the man he had taken to be one of the most obliging of his friends. Writing two years later, in the *Souvenirs d'Égotisme* he draws a very unpleasing portait of M. le Baron Mareste. There had not, he insists, ever been a genuine friendship between them. But had Mareste really allowed himself to jeer at Beyle's economies? It is more likely that theirs had been an intimacy which flourished best over the distance between Milan and Paris, and that Mareste's treachery broke a link beginning to wear thin. Beyle would have forgiven a man he respected or who charmed him.

There was no open break. To avoid breakfasting with Mareste, as he had been doing ever since he came back from Milan, he gave up the café de Rouen. They continued to meet, to talk, and for two or three years to write. As for Mme de Rubempré, her epitaph is the single line in *Brulard* where she figures, after: 'Angela Pietragrua a été catin sublime', as: 'Mme Azur catin non sublime'.

The pains of hurt vanity are sharp and biting. He had been stung. Surprisingly, less than eight weeks after his disillusionment he was reassured and soothed. Giulia Rinieri was a charming and uncommonly frank young Italian woman of good family, living in Paris with the seventy-year-old Daniello Berlinghieri, resident minister of Tuscany to the French court: he presented her as his niece: she may have been his daughter. Beyle had met her twice, once *chez* Cuvier, once at the legation. Abruptly, towards the end of January, she reappeared in his life, and in the manner of a determined young woman in a Shaw comedy threw herself at his head: 'Je sais bien,' she told him, 'et depuis longtemps que tu es vieux et laid.' Although she was offering him an assurance he needed all his life, he was mistrustful enough to keep her waiting until the third week in March before he became her lover.

During this year, his last in Paris for some time, he worked extremely hard. He published three admirable *nouvelles* in the *Revue de Paris* to which Delacroix had introduced him, one, *Vanina Vanini*, a vivid scrawl of Mathilde de la Mole. When did he go back to the manuscript of *Le Rouge et le Noir*? Possibly in mid-January. As one approaches this, the first of his two masterpieces, it will seem proper to use in speaking about them the name he had chosen for himself, as writer, in 1817. Not that the creatures of Beyle's imagination are greater than Beyle. That does not happen. He *is* Julien Sorel, Fabrice del Dongo, Count Mosca, Lucien Leuwen. He chose to put a narrow but perceptible distance between himself and his creation. So be it.

He was happy. 'J'étais parfaitement heureux, c'est trop dire mais enfin fort passablement heureux, quand j'écrivais *le Rouge et le Noir*.' (*Vie de Henri Brulard*) Very tolerably happy—it recalls the twitch of mockery in the corner of his mouth, very clear in the medallion David made of his head in 1829. Yet has any other writer experienced a more passionate, more acute pleasure in knowing that he is working at the height of his powers? Too much has been written about his projection of himself and his unfulfilled ambitions into his novels. The process is infinitely subtler: undeniably, on one level, the character of Julien Sorel is an outlet for his own half-bitter, half-arrogant sense that he was irremediably an outsider in his age and society, an exception: on another and deeper level, it is a hymn to energy, the quality he admired above all other human and social impulses; spontaneous violence in a man or woman drew him irresistibly, as though, in some visceral way, he envied it. His image of post-Napoleonic society is of one in which vital energies are repressed or sapped by political reaction, and independence of mind a sure way to neglect or worse: it is dangerous to think, still more dangerous to nourish ambitions which might disturb the existing order. None of his books is more acid in its portrait of an upper class in which charming well-mannered imbeciles are less numerous than cold-willed hypocrites and despots. And in none is his loathing of a middle class with no thoughts beyond fattening itself so ferocious.

In all this the contrast is with the Napoleonic era. Napoleon is everywhere in the book. Stendhal's attitude to him can seem equivocal: in fact it is intelligibly consistent. For the young soldier of 1796 idolised by a bullied rebellious child, the military genius carrying the virus of freedom across frontiers, he felt something nearer to worship than to the pride and self-satisfaction of the ordinary citizen of *la grande nation*: to the careerist of 1804, the dictator, the betrayer of the republican ideal, the creator of a police state, he was as hostile as Mme de Stael herself. Throughout his later life he turned two faces to Napoleon. The hostility was a rational reaction, the other a recurring nostalgia for youth, the freedom, excitement and hopes of an intoxicatedly happy young man in Italy, Napoleon's Italy, in 1800. Perhaps truer to say that Napoleon haunted his mind as the image of a dead man haunts friends and lovers, withdrawing, returning, undying because dead: 'La vieillesse de ceux d'entre nous qui ont vu la retraite de Moscou ne sera pas ridicule' (*Promenades dans Rome*, 1828) and, written in April 1837 in a preface to a second version of his never completed *Vie de Napoléon*: 'L'amour pour Napoléon est la seule passion qui me soit restée; ce qui ne m'empêche pas de voir les défauts de son esprit et les misérables faiblesses qu'on peut lui reprocher.'

He is not always so judicious about Napoleon, but this stands.

For Julien Sorel, intelligent, sensitive, in his rare moments of happiness a simple charming young creature, savagely bullied by his peasant father, Napoleon is God. His imagination has been inflamed by the stories told him by a survivor of Napoleon's 1796 campaign in Italy. His is the Napoleon of the legend, and the *Mémorial de Sainte Hélène*—a book 'for which he would have laid down his life'—his sole guide of belief and conduct. In 1830 the road Napoleon took was no longer open to young men without breeding or money; his only chance of advancement was through the priesthood, demanding from him not only to get himself an education of sorts, but to keep a watch on his every word and gesture in order to persuade his superiors that he could be trusted to behave discreetly. Already at eighteen, he was becoming an accomplished hypocrite. 'In the whole of his life he had never spoken sincerely except to the old Sergeant-Major.'

The moment when Stendhal saw that he could inject the Napoleonic myth into the story of a sordid crime turned his novel at a stroke into a great tragi-comedy.

At yet another level, Julien embodies Stendhal's profound conviction that the exceptional individual is always defeated by the pressures of society: the gross reality will wear down or kill his passionate energy the more surely if he has to start from the bottom in such a society as that of 1830. To create the portrait of a 'plebeian in revolt' demanded, and got, from Stendhal an imaginative leap. He endowed Julien with his own least manageable virtues, his hatred of authority and patronage, his hot-tempered pride, his quivering sensibility, but the circumstances that drive Julien, if he is to succeed in his ambition, to make his way by lying and dissembling, make him an 'exception' of an anything but Stendhalian kind. He has nothing of his creator's invincible gaiety, nothing, inevitably nothing, of Stendhal's scorn for hypocrisy and uncompromising understanding of himself. He does some things less forgivable, because calculated, than his obsessed attempt at killing. And he remains a quixotically heroic figure, and appealing.

None of this makes him a symbol of anything whatever: he exists, as himself, with an intense energy, a young peasant, a freak in his savagely harsh family, fastidious, with ambitions that burn him to the bone, capable of hatred and resentments, of depths of deceit, mistrust, and tenderness. The novel is a living organism, immensely complex. Into it are woven not only innumerable details in which Julien is narrowly Beyle himself—his loathing of Verrières and its inhabitants is Beyle's of Grenoble and the Dauphinois, his frozen silence in M. de Rênal's house that of an abashed sixteen-year-old in a Paris drawing-room, the spelling mistakes he makes in his first letters for M. de la Mole are those which brought Pierre Daru's fury down on young Beyle—and not only Beyle's prejudices, his anti-clericalism in the vitriolic description of Julien's seminary in Besançon, his dislike of respectable bigots, but his adolescent faith in the power of intelligence. Henri Beyle's practice of filling notebooks with analyses of character form the base of Stendhal's vast gallery of portraits and speculations on ideas and society. In every page of this novel (as in the *Chartreuse*, and the alas, oh alas, unfinished *Lucien Leuwen*) are fused the memories of a lifetime, not recalled so much as felt again to the quick, and evoked with superb economy and particularity.

He did not write of love, he wrote of his own love for many women. His imagination needed this rich humus of reality. The vivid minor characters owe everything to a dense weight of observation and meditation: the others, the large portraits, are improvised—invented as a scientist invents, by intuitions piercing through layers of knowledge and experience, composed as a great musician composes—from the stored-up emotions of the sensitive receiving and recording instrument he was.

Trying to pin down Stendhal's models is not strictly a waste of time. But to say that Mathilde de la Mole has traits taken from his faithless mistress, Alberthe de Rubempré, from Clémentine Curial, from Giulia Rinieri's youthful boldness, possibly from the escapades of a well-born young woman, Mary de Neuville, says little of moment. The important, the significant thing, is the fusion of memory and reverie, the confluence, at a great depth, of currents of feeling flowing into every minute, every incident, of the action. Mathilde de la Mole bears no resemblance to Mathilde Dembowski, but Henri Beyle's hopeless passion stains every thread of Julien's for both his women. The density of emotional experience on which this novel, like the others, draws, reaches back to a passionate child's love of his young mother and impotent rage against his father: at its deepest level Beyle's adult feeling for women is the same mingling of terror and ecstasy roused in a schoolboy by the sight of a young actress: all his passions, whether successful or barren, for the women whose initials he draws in the dust of the path above the lake of Albano in 1835, repeat the same gesture of mortal nervousness, stupidity, obsessive longing: the schemer, the cool seducer he liked to seem, with his absurd rules of strategy, shared the skin of an adolescent who needed nothing more than a glance to be made insanely happy or desperate. It is so with Julien, moved to tears by the genuine kindness of an old priest. One side of his double nature is an acute sensibility and a childish delight in the simplest pleasures. This note of innocent happiness is struck again and again through the book: it is a child, it is the child Henri, escaped for a few days from his oppressors, who chases butterflies in M. de Rênal's garden at Vergy, exults in his brief freedom in the mountains above Verrières, is enchanted by Mme de Rênal's dresses.

Julien's weeks in the condemned cell are serenely and purely happy; into them he crowds a lifetime of gentleness and meditation, a token not only of what he might have been if he had been born free and loved, but of that side of Henri Beyle himself which wanted to stand apart from the world, was defeated by his hungers and ambitions, and in its turn defeated them.

The distance between this novel and *Armance* is immense. He was now in full possession of his style. It is not easy for the reader who has once succumbed to it to find any other tolerable. Its clarity is deceptive, an illusion of the light striking through depth on depth of experience, its details remembered, re-imagined, with astonishing vividness and an infectious pleasure: it has the spontaneity of the finest talk, an air of perpetual improvisation arrived at by years of practice and hard-earned intimacy with the prose writers of the seventeenth and eighteenth centuries.

He had moments later when he thought that the writing in *Le Rouge et le Noir* might have been too abrupt, too unemotional, too dry. But he knew better: 'Je regarde et j'ai toujours regardé mes ouvrages comme des billets à la loterie. Je n'estime que d'être reimprimé en 1900.' At other moments he made it 1935. Either date will do.

Dry? Stendhal, whose every phrase is informed by controlled emotion! Find another writer able in four or five lines to evoke both the sound the heavy knife of a guillotine makes in falling and the exquisite serenity of a death willed and accepted with lucid simplicity.

Chapter 9

THE FIRST PART of his manuscript was in the publisher's hands in May. He continued to work strenuously over the book as a whole, adding a vast quantity of episodes, comments, observations, strokes of character, a prolonged re-working, revivifying, of the original version. As the proofs came in, he gave them the same attention, taking on himself the cost to the publisher of his ferocious energy. The process went on for some six months and might have lasted longer. Levavasseur was paying him one thousand five hundred francs, on which narrow margin of solvency he walked with his habitual insouciance. His letters to his friends during these months, Mlle Sophie, Sutton Sharpe, Mérimée, Mme Jules Gaulthier, are marvellously gay and witty.

His work, and that of the compositors, was interrupted by the three days of the July Revolution. The collapse of the drably repressive Bourbon government delighted him, though I doubt whether there was much depth to his qualified enthusiasm for Louis-Philippe. At forty-seven he had reached a point in his political thinking of half-ironical half-bored acceptance of a restricted monarchy as the best government to be had in a nation of well-born politicians ('Mon plat ami Félix Faure . . . Canaille! Canaille! Canaille!') and a greedy and abominably uncultivated middle class. He was that paradox, a born rebel against arbitrary authority with a distaste for disorder and indiscipline; passionate for social justice provided that it is achieved without corroding the quality of life: 'J'aime le peuple, je déteste ses oppresseurs, mais ce serait pour moi un supplice de tout les instants que de vivre avec le peuple.' He was fastidious to a fault. Very much the aristocrat, Mérimée said. Had had been born in a powerful family he would have been a democrat of the most dangerous sort; he believed in democracy without liking it.

A few months were long enough to disillusion him with Louis-Philippe.

Meantime, in August, he bestirred himself to try for a place in the new, possibly liberal government. He got an appointment to see Guizot, and laid his qualifications for the post of préfet before a minister infinitely too shrewd and rigid to trust either Beyle's constancy or his tongue.

He fell back to the idea of a consulate. Here he was on better ground. Better for a man whose friends, however genuinely attached, were for the most part inclined not to take his crises seriously. Domenico di Fiore and Mme Victor de Tracy were close to the Minister for Foreign Affairs: both assured him that he would be listened to with sympathy if he applied. There is something touching in his letter to Comte Molé, the flicker of self-mockery behind the careful approach: he was not amused, he was in real need. 'M. Beyle, pénetré de reconnaisance qu'on le trouve bon encore à quelque chose, malgré ses 47 ans et ses 14 ans de service, expose qu'il est absolument sans fortune. Son père s'est ruiné à 73 ans. M. Beyle désirerait une place de consul général à Naples, Gênes, Livourne . . . Si le Consulat est trop au-dessus de ce qu'on paraît avoir la bonté de vouloir faire pour lui, il demanderait la place de premier secrétaire à Naples ou à Rome. . . .'

Without doubt Beyle owed his appointment as consul at Trieste to Mme Victor de Tracy's impeccably delicate and intelligent use of her husband's connections with Molé. He knew it. 'Je lui devrait *tout*,' he said, 'tout simplement.'

He was thankful to be placed at last, but sorry it had to be Trieste—*in mezzo ai barbari*. He invited friends, Sainte-Beuve, Delacroix, to visit him. How was he going to get through the evenings? Trieste was not Italy.

He left Paris on 6 November, before *Le Rouge et le Noir* was published, carrying with him a letter of introduction from Sophie Duvaucel to a distinguished lady in Venice which indiscreetly he read, and roared with laughter at the epithets Mlle Sophie had found for him: 'L'un des hommes les plus spirituels et les plus aimables de Paris.' Before leaving he wrote to Daniello Berling-hieri, asking to be allowed to marry his niece. The polite answer he got was in effect a refusal. Had he, having been very candid about his lack of means, expected anything else? Was it a relief? His letter has a ring of sincerity—almost of humility: 'J'ai besoin d'être rassuré par elle. . . .' To suppose that when he wrote it he was in a mood to settle down with a young woman in whose kindness for him he trusted does not rule out the possibility, say the likelihood, that to be rejected was also, other things considered, a relief.

Le Rouge et le Noir came out a week after he left. The critics, including the eminent critic of the *Journal des Débats*, Jules Janin, felt impelled to give it a good deal of attention and, to avenge themselves for the outrage to their sensibilities, little praise: as did his friends, they condemned it as barbarously uncouth, a verdict which a contemporary reader, struck above all by the spontaneity and lightness of the writing, finds singularly obtuse. Mérimée's letter of December 1830, sent to Trieste, was no more brutally frank than he would have been in conversation. 'Il y a dans le caractère de Julien des traits atroces dont tout le monde sent la vérité, mais qui font horreur. Le but de l'art n'est pas de montrer ce côté de la nature humaine. Rappellez-vous le portrait de Delia par Swift, et l'abominable vers qui le termine: *But Delia pisses and Delia shits*. Certes, mais pourquoi le dire? Vous êtes plein de ces vérités-là. . . .' He ends his letter on an anecdote about the young Spanish queen quite unspeakably odious, worthy of—no matter.

It is not to be supposed that Beyle was wholly indifferent to the rejection by friends and critics of a book he knew to be the finest thing he had done. That he was not cast down, or not seriously, is less courage than stubbornness, a stubbornness in which it is not hard to recognise a trace of Chérubin Beyle's persistence in ruin-ing himself with his agricultural experiments. One does not, if one is a Beyle, pursue with less pleasure and energy the passion, or obsession, of a lifetime for no better reason than that it continues to be a series of checks.

He reached Trieste on 5 November, with a light purse and modestly few possessions, determined to convince authority of his competence in action: he was not, after all, an amateur as an administrator. He began to occupy himself at once, discreetly. Until the Austrian government sent the exequatur—his authorisation as consul—he had no status. He became anxious and, starved of conversation in the evenings, very bored. Trieste was a lively handsome city, but there was a horrible wind, and the cold gripped his bowels. To distract himself he paid a brief visit to Fiume, and in December to Venice, where he had friends, a café in the Piazza San Marco, and above all the Fenice and music. It was the day after he came back that he heard he had been turned down: in fact Metternich had already, in November, asked Paris to provide a less undesirable consul. Momentarily dismayed, he wrote to Mme Victor de Tracy, and even, asking him to talk to Apollinaire d'Argout, to Mareste. When, after a brief delay, he was told of his transfer to Civitavecchia, he was relieved and more than a little resentful. Not only was it, compared to Trieste, a small dull hole of a port, but he was dropping a third of his salary: ten thousand francs against fifteen. He felt disgraced. The one merit the place had was its nearness to Rome. Hoping to spend half the month there—surely not too much to concede to a poor devil of forty-eight, 'triste débris de la campagne de Russie et de dix autres . . .'— he asked Argout to commend him to the newly-appointed French ambassador, 'pour qu'il *ne me fasse de mal*'.

It was March when he left Trieste and travelled through Florence and Bologna in the wake of a confused insurrection against the papal power. He made notes of everything he saw and everything he could learn and from Florence sent four long immensely detailed political reports to the Foreign Minister, Comte Sebastiani. Enormously pleased with them, he ignored the possibility that members of the Foreign Office staff would be outraged by his presumption—indeed the danger did not even occur to him. He intended to stretch his duties as consul to keep the office thoroughly informed on the social and political state of his, so to speak, diocese: he had been away from the milieu too long to realise his total irrelevance in that world. Warned, later, by an affectionate and exasperated Mlle Sophie to abstain—For heaven's sake, she wrote, be sensible, don't discuss things you have no business to be putting your nose into. Content yourself with reports on the movement of ships in and out of Civitavecchia. When will you learn?—he abstained. Regretfully.

He reached Civitavecchia on the 17th of April, in the evening. Italy and a spring evening. Surely, if only for a moment, he felt a lift of the heart, half memory, half sensuous pleasure.

Four days after his arrival he went to Rome, presented himself at the embassy and was received by the Comte de Sainte-Aulaire with exquisite politeness and gentleness. He was immensely relieved, he felt he had a friend.

His nomination had been agreed, reluctantly, by Cardinal Bernetti. Not that the papal authorities approved of him, or ever did: throughout his whole period of office the police kept an alert eye on him, in Civitavecchia, in Rome: he was spied on, his letters opened. He took precautions. At the start he had other worries: he fell ill in Rome the day after he went there, quite seriously ill, an intestinal inflammation, and did not get back to his post until early May, still good for nothing. Sainte-Aulaire advised him to go to Albano, and he spent the second half of June at Castelgandolfo. Ten thousand nightingales, he told Domenico di Fiore, splendid trees, two unbelievable lakes, a forest, and a hill he was still too weak to climb.

He had found tolerable lodgings in Civitavecchia, with a wide view over the harbour and the open sea, which he enjoyed looking at. What other amusements had he? A small theatre. Lark and quail shooting. He lost no time in making precisely the sort of friends the authorities had expected of him, a cultivated antiquary, Donato Bucci, who presented him to two other undesirable characters, Pietro Manzi, a classical scholar and archaeologist, and the barrister Benedetto Blazi, a music lover. All three, like Beyle's friends in Milan, were liberals. They were the salt of his life in Civitavecchia, otherwise without savour. His post was no sinecure. He had eleven vice-consulates in his charge; they entangled him in a vast correspondence, too much of it with the vice-consul of Ancona, whose stubborn refusal to grasp the most elementary

facts of finance shows a touch of genius. There were few excitements: early in his second year he was handed a difficult mission
involving French troops sent to Ancona as a warning that France
did not take lightly the arrival of Austrian troops in the Papal
States, and carried out his very delicate duties with so much skill
and tact that Sainte-Aulaire wrote to Paris demanding for M.
Beyle the cross of the Légion d'honneur. It had been a sore point
with Beyle for a long time that he had not had the cross for the
Russian campaign or for the administration of the duchy of
Brunswick. To be ignored as of no importance humiliated him—
almost the only symptom of vanity to be noticed in him, and
hardly worth noticing.

He went to Rome whenever he could find an excuse; and in
July, when he was convalescent, arranged to share a flat there with
a friend, a celebrated Genevese painter he had known in Paris.
Almost the same age, Abraham Constantin was sensible, calm,
upright, responsible, a good man, to be confidently trusted, one of
the kindest friends Beyle ever had. They shared the same tastes in
music and art, and the same salons. There is a touch of womanly
solicitude in Constantin's care of his friend: writing to ask his
brother to send two gold watch-chains, he is careful to stress that
the chain intended for Beyle must be from four to six inches the
longer, to allow for his great girth.

What Rome offered Beyle was a semblance of the things he
could not live without: cafés, a little intelligent conversation, not
enough, some not very good music, and—he never changed—
women's caressing disturbing smiles. He was quite extraordinarily
lucky in his ambassador. From the start Sainte-Aulaire treated him
not as the consul, an underling from whom he expected satisfaction, but as a valued friend: he was a constant guest in the
countess's salon, expected at all the dinner-parties, private and
ambassadorial. He had Sainte-Aulaire's full backing not only
against the efforts of the papal authorities to get rid of him but
against officials in Paris: he was grateful on both counts. So far as
Roman society is concerned, one may doubt whether he had ever
seriously expected that he would dwindle into a consul. Nor did

he. Famous doors were open to him, from the Caetani palace to the Villa Médicis where the director of the French Academy in Rome, the painter Horace Vernet, entertained more simply. Away from his consulate he became the connoisseur of Italian history and art, delighted to tell distinguished visitors—some of whom, Count Alexander Tourgenev for one, knew to whom they were privileged to listen—what to admire in churches, galleries, ruins, and to spend two days or two weeks on their education. All this was pleasurable enough. But Rome was not Paris, and the talk in salons and at dinner had nothing of the intellectual energy and wit of evenings *chez* Gérard, *chez* Madame Ancelot, *chez* M. de Tracy, and the rest. The endless complaints of authority of his imprudent tongue were not groundless: imprudence was his capital fault. He felt more and more out of his own world.

Here if anywhere is the place to recall the spitefully amused letter Mareste wrote to Sutton Sharpe in London on 6 August 1831. 'Beyle est consul à Civitavecchia. J'ai vu ces jours-ci Horace Vernet, directeur de l'Académie de Peinture à Rome; il m'a dit que le grand homme s'ennuyait outrageusement dans la Ville Eternelle. Il veut parler librement comme dans nos salons à Paris; il discute, il tranche, il disserte à sa manière. Les pauvres Romains, qui ont une peur horrible de se compromettre avec leur aimable gouvernement, se bouchent les oreilles et s'enfuient. L'interlocuteur reste seul et il ne sait que devenir. Vous savez que pour lui un auditoire est chose nécessaire. . . .'

In Henri Beyle boredom was an active state. Mérimée said of him, without irony, that he never learned how to be bored; the tiresomeness of a dull fellow struck him as pure malice, and what he felt for a bore was savage hatred.

True enough. And where his own life was in question boredom took the form of outraged impatience with all that came between him and the one aim he never or very rarely lost sight of, his obstinate will to become, by hard work, by absorbing the most illustrious studies of human nature, by looking coolly into himself, a great writer. Again and again, in pursuit of his aim, one sees him taken by a decision rather than taking it. The decision to reject the Polytechnique, to abandon the career Pierre Daru held out to him and get back to his attic, to go to Milan in 1814. It was as an essential part of his discipline as a writer that he sought the intense happiness he got from music and paintings, some musicians, some painters, from certain landscapes, from the excitement of ruthlessly frank talk.

Civitavecchia bored him, Rome bored him, though less. He alarmed and dismayed his friends in Paris, particularly the devoted Romain Colomb, by writing to them of his furious wish to leave. It was not in Colomb's sober nature to credit that whatever grounds authority had for complaining of his tongue Beyle was in fact a good consul and gave the fullest satisfaction to his chief in Rome. All he could suppose was that a restless maladroit Beyle was meditating some folly or other. At any cost he must keep his post. To throw it up, risking poverty and a miserable old age in Paris—madness. . . . And so on and so forth. No doubt, too, this was the common opinion among Beyle's friends, who for all their affection were not anxious to have an unemployed Beyle on their hands.

In fact he had no intention of becoming, at his age, unemployed: the Dauphinois in him saw to that. What he wanted was to get away from the boredom of Civitavecchia, 'pays ennuyeux comme la peste'. To get away, get another post. Perhaps Leghorn. He seized every chance to travel. He was more at his ease in Naples and Florence than in Rome, and between August 1831 and January 1834 he paid five visits to Florence. He was at home here in the cafés and restaurants, and in Vieusseux's celebrated literary and scientific library where he met and talked with the cultivated liberal intellectuals of the city: he had friends among them with whom he dined. He knew Leopardi. After the dullness of Roman society Florence intoxicated him.

He took his consular work seriously—without for a moment considering it as other than a duty, like the duty to keep up appearances in his social life. But even at the end of a year, when he had familiarised himself with a fairly demanding routine, he could not dream of attempting a major novel. Writing to di Fiore in June 1832, he told him: 'J'ai eu une attaque de goutte au pied droit; approche de la cinquantaine; du reste, le cœur plus ferme que jamais. . . . Quand je suis exilé ici, j'écris l'histoire de mon dernier voyage à Paris, de juin 1821 à novembre 1830. Je m'amuse à décrire toutes les faiblesses de l'animal; je ne l'épargne nullement.' He is talking of *Souvenirs d'Égotisme*. No writer, except Montaigne, possibly except Jules Renard, has regarded himself with so calm a detachment, such complete lack of vanity, whether the vanity of modest self-deprecation or the vanity of unabashed frankness. He was writing for his own pleasure, a writer in the habit of examining himself not merely coldly—which is not, with practice, too difficult—but with justice, even with liking. As he wrote of them he relived the nine years, enjoyed his morning coffee and brioches in the café de Rouen, walked smilingly into drawing-rooms, turned an edged gaiety on his friends, and in silence endured the sharpness of his grief for Métilde.

It is an enchantingly witty book, lucid and mocking, like the finest, least emphatic conversation. You need not take *au pied de la lettre* everything he thinks fit to tell us, but the fugitive scenes and portraits give pleasure of a rare kind. His pen raced, he wrote at a gallop. He is describing the life of a man he knew too clearly to be surprised by him—and after fifteen days he stopped. Why? One of the so many things the most ruthlessly honest of writers did not tell us about himself.

In September he began a novel he called *Une Position sociale*; again he threw it aside, after three chapters. It was not among the functions of a consul to draw a portrait of the political and social activities of diplomatic circles in Rome, of the French embassy, its ambassador, his seductively charming and elegant wife and her relations with the author in the person of M. Roizand. Certainly he intended to make use of them, but later.

For one reason or another he did not spend a leave in Paris until the autumn of 1833. Then he took three months. It was a return not only to what he thought of as civilised life but a return in time: the same dinners with Mérimée, Sutton Sharpe, Mareste,

Delacroix, di Fiore, and other familiars; the same salons, Mme Ancelot on Tuesday, Dr Edwards or Baron Gérard on Wednesday, and the rest of them. Not quite the same: the great Cuvier had died, but Mme Cuvier and Mlle Sophie Duvaucel received his and their friends each Saturday as before. And as before, in the rue d'Anjou, Mme Victor de Tracy and her unfailing benevolence: too heavy a word for her affection for him: he interested her, amused her, and she felt a responsibility for him as for an engaging, brilliant and insecure member of the family.

In his friendship with Mme Jules Gaulthier there had been from the start liking and dependence on her sympathy and, given the warmth of his liking, and his distance from her, he fell easily into teasing endearments. Writing from Rome earlier this year, in May, he told her: 'J'ai pris la plume dans un transport d'amour pour vous. Tâchez, aimable Jules, d'avoir un pareil transport.' It was not an avowal, even lighthearted: more a half-mocking half provocatively affectionate smile. Since she was still living out at Saint-Denis she did not see much of him, if she saw anything, during his three months of pleasures to be snatched up again, familiar salons, a visit to Mme Curial at her country house, male dinner-parties, the opera. Soon after he arrived she sent him the manuscript of a long novel she had written, on which she wanted advice. He had no time to look at it, and when he left to go back to Civitavecchia he took it with him, promising to read it and write to her.

He left Paris on 4 December. At Lyon he took the Rhône boat to Marseille, and found George Sand with Alfred de Musset on board, they too on their way to Italy. The only account of the three-day voyage is hers, in her *Histoire de ma vie*. She was interested by Beyle, even amused, but his excitable buffoonery during the evening they spent ashore at a small hotel in Bourg-Saint-Andéol offended her: so, when he passed from caustic mockery to indecency, did his talk. Did he suppose he was pleasing her by treating her as if she were masculine enough not to be shocked by hair-raising impropriety? He misjudged her. There was no need for him to defend himself against the malice and affectation of a female author. She possessed neither. She was highly intelligent

---

SPEAKING OF STENDHAL

rather than original, intellectually masculine, with a man's features, and the emotions of a woman, not vain, not loose-living, not pretentious: he could safely have trusted her with his true dislikes and sympathies. For all her displeasure she recognised coolly that there was something exceptional about him, a quality other and rarer than talent. What is better she saw through him. 'Mais je ne crois pas qu'il fût méchant,' she decided shrewdly: 'il se donnait trop de peine pour le paraître.' Which says everything for him and much for her.

She was none the less frankly glad to see the back of him at Marseille. He went on alone, by coach, to Italy and his consulate, delaying for a week in Florence on the way, long enough to write to Paris, to the Foreign Minister, a long letter of precisely the kind he had been warned not to write.

In March this year Saint-Aulaire was replaced by the Marquis de la Tour-Maubourg: Beyle had lost a friend, but the new ambassador was indulgent and courteous and so far as he could took little notice of complaints from Paris of his volatile consul's absences from his post; and Beyle continued to be a consul like no other, highly efficient in a delicate situation or an emergency, firm and tactful with Francophobe papal officials, and to live in Rome as often as possible. In Paris, so long as the Duc de Broglie was at the Foreign Office he had a friendly minister. Whether because they had known each other when both were auditors to the Conseil d'État, or because Beyle's indiscreet letters were some use to him, Victor de Broglie seems to have allowed, even encouraged him to write about the political situation in Rome, its scandals and intrigues, with complete freedom. No other Foreign Minister, neither Thiers nor Guizot, would have permitted it: he did not attempt it with them. When this year Broglie was replaced for some months by the Comte de Rigny, the complaints of negligence became a torrent. He had an Iago in the office in Civitavecchia in the person of his chief clerk, a Greek named Lysimaque Tavernier, whom he had kept on in spite of being warned by the outgoing consul that the fellow was sly and disloyal. It was an error of kindness he paid for when after a brief period of seeming devotion

128

Lysimaque began denouncing him to the papal authorities as an atheist, a radical and a French agent, and blackguarding him in Paris as often as without danger to himself he could. Obsequious and, more to the point, a thoroughly competent official, he was able to persuade the Marquis de la Tour-Maubourg that he was both zealous and indispensable, and Beyle's efforts to get rid of him foundered on the ambassador's shrewd reminder that he was able to spend as much time as he did in Rome only because his clerk was so efficient. And don't delude yourself, he added; you might make up your mind to live in Civitavecchia, but you wouldn't be able to stand it. Beyle submitted, and the treacherous Greek remained to plague him, and his successor after him. It is pleasant to recall that he did not achieve his ambition to occupy Beyle's chair and ended, eight years after Beyle's death, as consul in Baghdad.

Beyle was ageing and hated it: he had gout, and the hard use he made of his eyes, reading into the small hours, now forced spectacles on him. He was more and more bored with Rome. Four years of solitude with learned fools who took a quarter of an hour to answer, he told di Fiore, were stupefying him. Even the cross of the Légion d'honneur, received at last, in January 1835, gave him less pleasure than it should have done, though he was far from being as indifferent as he took care to seem. To his friends in Paris he continued to be an object of anxiety and the half impatient sympathy roused by a man who has not the tact to acquiesce pleasantly in defeat. His cousin Colomb, the last person to appreciate that without intelligent talk, almost without music, he was morally starved, warned him severely that his efforts to get another post might well end in his losing his employment altogether. A pleasant letter Mérimée wrote him in reply to demands for advice suggested Spain; Valencia for charming women, Barcelona if he must have conversation: but, writing about their restless friend to Mlle Sophie, he remarked drily that in fact Beyle's only choice lay between accepting his inglorious life in a small port or Paris again, at the mercy of editors, 'bien pauvre existence par le temps qui court'. An existence Mérimée himself did not dream of attempting.

The truth, or a sensible part of it, was that Beyle's passion for Italy was wearing threadbare: he longed desperately for Paris. Domenico di Fiore got most of his laments, the frankest. The letter written to him from Civitavecchia in April 1835 ends: 'La petite chambre avec cinq francs de revenu et cinq francs gagnés par un roman, serait le bonheur suprême. Je suis fait pour vivre avec deux bougies et une écritoire, et maintenant en vous écrivant je suis heureux ainsi. . . . Adieu, j'ai envie de me pendre, et de tout quitter pour une chambre au cinquième étage, rue Richepanse.' Yet he knew himself too well not to know that he was exasperating himself with a passing nostalgia for the shabby room, uncertain income, and endless time to read and write which were all an eighteen-year-old needed to be supremely happy. He could not return to poverty in an attic, he had not even the strength that had kept him going during the last years at 71 rue de Richelieu.

It would be ludicrous to imagine that he was continually depressed. That, as he would have said, was not one of the animal's habits. He contrived to amuse himself even in Civitavecchia. Eight miles inland were Etruscan excavations, and with his friend Pietro Manzi he took an active share in them to the point during one season of employing six Neapolitan workers at a day's wage of twenty-odd sous, and acquired vases he gave to friends in Paris. In Rome he had taken a room for himself on the third floor of the Conti palazzo. He kept it until his next leave, occupying it for weeks at a time: large parts of *Lucien Leuwen* and the *Vie de Henry Brulard* were written here. Abraham Constantin lodged a few steps away; they spent the evenings together, contentedly enough, dined, taking their time over it, then moved to the wooden benches of a café in the Piazza Novena: there was wine, and figs, and after the heat of the day a little freshness in the close air. He had other friends in Rome with whom, though not intellectually stretched, he was at ease: and music heard in the house of a hospitable lawyer may at moments have disturbed the dust on his past; his host's wife had sung at the Scala.

He had become a familiar of the eminent Cini family, respected, liked, cossetted in their country house at Castelgandolfo, and in

Rome. The adolescent in his gross body was capable to the very last of being moved by a young smiling Comtesse Cini, or by the talented young actress at the théâtre Vallé who let him flirt with her for an hour between scenes. Behind the vivacious or maliciously smiling mask of the social Beyle was a man conscious of ageing, of disappointed ambitions, of fiascos, of his corpulence and his baldness, and grateful for what only the friendship of women gave him, an emotion between sensual attraction and tenderness.

Need it be said that he was still as certain of his immortality as the young man preparing himself to be the greatest of poets? He had not been back from leave longer than four months when he began a new long novel. He had read Jules Gaulthier's manuscript and on 4 May wrote to her about it, not at great length but as seriously and unsparingly as he would have criticised one of his male friends. Did she, as in an enchanting reply, characteristically modest, she said she would, try to follow his advice? No matter: the manuscript is lost. His imagination had snatched up the living fragments of her theme; in three or four days, not more, of exultantly hard labour he had laid out the ossature of a novel in which the violently broken love affair is no more, and no less, than the kernel of a superb political and social portrait of the July monarchy. He worked as he had always worked, absorbed, planning, re-planning, revising each chapter, each line, adding, adding: a seemingly inexhaustible flow of memory and imagination. He gave the whole of his leisure to it, in Rome and Civitavecchia. There were to have been three parts of *Lucien Leuwen*. In the first, set in the garrison town of Nancy, a young subaltern as unworldly and impulsive, as vulnerable, as the young Beyle, but handsome, slender, and well-off, the son of a Parisian banker, makes his way into the aristocratic society, ultra-conservative, ultra-Catholic, of the place, so stiff-necked that it acknowledges allegiance only to a king living in Prague—a gallery of provincial portraits of a delicious dry liveliness. These chapters are full of enchanting things: the wit and spontaneity of the talk—echoes of Paris and Milan in the heavy silence of Civitavecchia—the delicacy and tenderness of the love scenes, the young gaiety, the music of horns in the forest outside Nancy, the energy and candour with which Lucien throws himself at life: he has traits of that Victor Jacquemont who died young, his natural charm, his equally natural seriousness, his involuntary frankness and honesty. Of course he falls hopelessly and passionately in love. Bathilde de Chasteller is another of Métilde's spectral doubles, as lovely and well-bred, as high minded—but kinder. The farcically unpleasant disruption of the affair drives him back to Paris, where his influential father gets him a position as secretary in the Ministry of the Interior. There follows the second part; a brilliantly savage exposure of the Orléanist régime: corruption, delations, police brutality, crooked elections, and a fine ironic account of the education of a quixotic and intelligent young man in the tortuousness of politics. Unlike Julien Sorel in the same Parisian world Lucien has not to struggle against a wounding sense of social inferiority. He matures; and keeps his integrity. 'Will you,' his father had asked him cynically, 'have the courage to become a scoundrel?'

As in all his novels Stendhal shares the stage with his characters. His attitude to Napoleon, admiration corrected by mistrust, is Lucien's, to whom he gives as well his involuntary dislike for democracy, the distaste of a fanatical republican who disliked America because he was horrified by the idea of having to seek the favour of uneducated workers and plebeian bigots 'as at Philadelphia', and whose fastidious skin shrank from the unwashed and ill-bred, while he wanted vehemently to see the lower classes free and happy, and believed that they alone were a source of energy in a world of swinish bourgeois and selfish aristocrats. It is not impossible that the harshness of the criticism Lucien makes of the régime hides some unformulated uneasiness Beyle felt about having sought shelter in it.

His progress was interrupted by bouts of illness: early in May 1835 he was seriously ill, fever and gout, too ill during some weeks to get himself to Albano into cooler air. Recovered, he began writing again. And suddenly, at some moment in November, stopped. The third part exists only as a mass of plans, notes, drafts: left almost penniless by his father's abrupt death, Lucien was to be posted to an embassy (which could only be Rome, whether he called it Madrid or 'Capel'), have an unfortunate affair with the wife of the ambassador, be dismissed, and reconciled in some way with his Bathilde.

Why did he stop? Trouble with the plot? The absurd incident of Mme de Chasteller's false pregnancy is not the single part of the book where his uncertain inventive ingenuity misled him. She had, too, become a shadowy figure on the margin of the Parisian scene. Could he have revived her? It is highly unlikely that there was only one reason why he abandoned a novel to which he had given so much care and energy. One very obvious reason offers itself: as with *Une Position sociale* he must sooner or later have reflected on the indiscretion of an account of French diplomatic circles, coming from him. A reason he himself gives is that a third volume filled with completely new characters would be implausible. All no doubt true and relevant, but possibly not the truth.

He was bored. Bored by the spiritless vacuity of Roman society —no decent music, and salons so dull they were not worth the trouble of getting oneself there. And, I must believe, by the conditions under which he was writing the most demanding book he had attempted since he came to Civitavecchia, finding it after nineteen months increasingly tedious to write in broken intervals, even the extended intervals allowed him by an ambassador who may have become willing to think of him as a writer first and a consul occasionally.

Boredom—'le seul malheur . . .'. In any form, the one mortal ill against which Henri Beyle had no defence except flight.

In October he had taken part of his manuscript to Ravenna with him, but in the three or four weeks he spent there did not touch it. Another idea, not new—he had had it already, more than once— took possession of him, and with overwhelming relief he abandoned the frustrating task *Leuwen* had become and, back in Rome, plunged into the *Vie de Henry Brulard*.

There may have been a brief period in his life, say the first ten years until he was handed over to what he calls 'l'affreuse tyrannie Raillane', before he began consciously to observe himself and others, without, be it said, at any stage, then or later, becoming in an ill sense self-conscious, and without ceasing to identify self-knowledge with happiness. In his speculative curiosity there is no trace of vanity. Irony, an irony not devoid of a flicker of half-amused tenderness, but no putting himself in a good light. All autobiography is distorted, the writer is looking inward at a figurant who is himself, is recalling joys and agonies which are in a significant sense done with. The fresco, as Stendhal himself says, is partly obliterated; there are vivid fragments. One catches sight here of the great Stendhalian paradox: how to reconcile his profound horror of being *deviné*, the pains he took to hide even from intimates his humiliations, disappointments, moments of searing anguish, with the smiling but ruthless exposure of his follies in this book. From the beginning he intended to leave the manuscript to be published after his death. Did he at a deep level *want*, provided he was out of reach, deaf, blind, to be seen for what he was? A deep human need, acute even in the man whose adolescent and adult life was spent in the double effort of exploring and guarding himself? A finally irresistible impulse to leave a mark, an image, even if it is rejected?

But notice that in the end he has kept us at a clear distance. Whether or not he meant, in this one of his books, to lay himself bare to our scrutiny, in fact he tells us infinitely less than, say, the complacent Gide. An excess of light falls on certain scenes and emotions, dazzling us: only in retrospect do we catch the undertones of Mozartian sadness in the energy and gaiety.

He had begun the writing on 23 November and for four months, whether in Rome or Civitavecchia, he gave it all the time not demanded by his consulate, writing with intense delight, in an increasingly illegible hand. It is unfinished, yes, covering only his first nineteen years, but in the digressions, the swift glances forward and back, the whole landscape of his life lies open, a chiaroscura of light and impenetrable darkness, the bright rays picking out a room, the side of a hill, a face, the rest left in obscurity. His peremptory care is to tell the truth about an ungovernable child and a young man who was a cauldron of energies. He wrote in feverish haste, with the same sort of pleasure it gave him to walk for the first time into a strange town where no one knew him. The impulse to discover himself, to set down without complaisance his hidden motives, ambitions, errors, unavowable desires, is doubled by the pleasure of abandoning himself to reverie, to the half charmed, half mocking contemplation of a life involuntarily divided between imagination and reason. From the famous opening on that magnificently sunny morning in Rome when he realises that he is within three months of being fifty—forgivably disingenuous, since he was fifty-two when, in 1835 (not, as he says, in 1832) he started—he has himself lucidly in view. 'Qu'ai-je été, que suis-je, en vérité je serais bien embarrassé de le dire. Je passe pour un homme de beaucoup d'esprit et fort insensible, roué même, et je vois que j'ai été constamment occupé par des amours malheureuses.' He judges himself without pity even for the stubborn often unhappy child or the just as stubborn adolescent, imprudent to the edge of ruining himself, avid for fame, secretive and frank, wildly happy and blackly unhappy for the lightest reasons.

Even during these months Paris gnawed him. Writing to Jules Gaulthier from Civitavecchia in March 1836 he cried: 'Dites-moi si un chat est mort dans votre rue. Ce sont les petits détails qui me sont précieux.' In February he had asked the Duc de Broglie for two months sick leave, to help him shake off the fevers he said he suffered in the bad air of Civitavecchia. It was granted five weeks later—by Thiers, who had replaced Broglie as Foreign Minister.

Enraptured, he scrawled a few notes in the margin of his manuscript, and on the 8th of April closed it forever, on a young man riding into Milan on a spring morning in June 1800. Would he, if he had lived longer than he did, have gone back to it? I think not. It is deeply right that it ends as it does, in a great cry of joy— 'Comment peindre le bonheur fou?' As in Le Rouge et le Noir when Julien touches briefly a height of triumph or in the instant before the guillotine drops, he knew, with the instinct of the dramatist he worked so hard to become, when not to trust words. The cry of joy *is* the end.

He left Rome on 11 May 1836. He was in Marseille three days later, and in Paris on the 24th and walking into the hôtel de la Paix, 17 rue de Mont-Blanc.

Chapter 10

THIERS DID NOT like him, nor he Thiers. They had known each other a long time, at least since 1822, when on Sunday afternoons they met in Étienne Delécluze's apartment. The future historian and statesman, then a journalist of the liberal persuasion, struck Beyle as a pompous bore and a bad clumsy writer, a judgement he naturally—his nature—made mockingly clear. Would he have behaved with more prudence if he had imagined a time when he would suffer from M. Thiers' extreme disapproval of a consul he considered lightminded and unreliable? Probably not. But for Mme de Tracy's friendship with the head of the Political Department of the Foreign Office he would scarcely have survived in Paris as long as September of his first year, when Thiers was replaced as Foreign Minister by Comte Molé, who liked and sympathised with this highly unusual subordinate: very certainly he would not have been able, as in one way or another he was, to stretch his three months to as many years, in fact until Molé resigned in 1839. Molé, 'aussi plat que possible', Mérimée said of him, writing to Sutton Sharpe. Maybe—but he was a good friend to Henri Beyle.

He had to live cheaply. Apart from his half-pay as consul he had only his narrow private income of military pension and annuity, some two thousand francs, a third of which went to Pauline. Even adding the far from famous sums earned in 1838 by the *Mémoires d'un Touriste* and the *nouvelles* published in the *Revue des deux Mondes*, it was a meagre total and forced the strictest economy on him. Did he do some work for Molé? He says so, but offers no details: it can hardly have been important. So much of his life after he first left Grenoble had been lived on a financial edge: he was used to it; he calculated carefully and during these years managed not only to live in Paris the social life of his wide acquaintance in intellectual, artistic and literary circles but—an enduring need of his restless mind—to travel.

He snatched up again familiar habits: uninterrupted hours of writing: salons where the conversation was gay and informed, music: on successive evenings in this first season he had the fierce intoxication of listening to the *Matrimonio segreto* and *Don Giovanni*; suppers at the café Anglais with Mérimée, di Fiore, Delacroix, Mareste—rarely more than eight persons, with or without the company of attractive easy young creatures from the theatre and the Opéra. For all the difference in their fortunes his relations with Mérimée were as close as they had been during the years after Milan, and he depended on the younger more successful writer for many of his pleasures, intellectual and social. But not as he depended on Domenico di Fiore: all his tenderness for this friend comes out in the letter he wrote from Rome on 19 April 1841 (and could not have written to any other of his small circle of intimates): 'Mais enfin je veux vous faire mes adieux, pour le cas où cette lettre serait l'ultima. *Je vous aime réellement et il n'y a pas foule.* . . .' And not as he depended on Romain Colomb, for whom he had the affection one can feel for the familiar furniture of a house: no one deserved it more than this grave somewhat solemn man who after Beyle died did everything to make safe his future as writer. Had it been left to Mérimée or even to Louis Crozet (who advised leaving *Le Rouge et le Noir* and the *Mémoires d'un Touriste* out of the first collected edition) it would have fared less well.

It was to Mérimée's friendship with the Comtesse de Montijo— one of the calm enduring friendships Mérimée formed with certain older very civilised women—that he owed one of his most completely satisfying pleasures during these years. Mme de Montijo was living in Paris with her two daughters, Francisca, known as Paca, and Eugénie; they took to Beyle at once, as very young children will to an adult who has no impulse to treat them otherwise than as small equals: on his frequent visits to the house they sat one on each knee and listened, absorbed, to tales of Napoleon's battles, vividly recalled by one of them when, as Empress of

France, she was alone in Paris on the eve of a later war. A year and a half before he died he had written to her in Madrid—she was then eleven or twelve—promising to send her the *Histoire du siège de Florence en 1530*, and giving her sound advice on preparing occupations for her old age. Did she recall that, too, again in Madrid at the end of her long life?

Something not to be forgotten about Henri Beyle is the instinctive respect and affection he roused in many well-bred intelligent women too sensible or too fastidious to fall in love with him, women such as Alexandrine Daru, Mme Victor de Tracy, Mlle Sophie Duvaucel, Mme Beugnot, the old Comtesse de Tascher, who reproved him when she thought he needed it, Mme Jules Gaulthier. During these years he saw a good deal of Mme Gaulthier. She was intelligent, charming, and at 46 still very attractive, and he was immensely fond of her: it rested with her to allow a warm friendship to dwindle into a liaison. He did, on one of his visits to her at Saint-Denis, make her a declaration. She was touched, and perhaps conscious that she was a little to blame, but she was too wise, too sharply aware of the simplicity of his heart, too spiritually fine and too fond of him to permit a clumsy error. He can have received few letters, I would think none, of such gentleness, delicate wit, and deeply sincere affection as the one she sent after him when he left the house.

He was infinitely more fortunate in his friends than in his lovers.

They were happy years, these between 1836 and 1839. Was he ever so happy again? He had never worked harder, or enjoyed it more, his attention caught by one project after another, or by two or three at once. It is not easy to keep track of him.

How long had the mirage of a life of Napoleon waited for him to attend to it? At least twenty years. In Milan in 1817, exasperated by Mme de Stael's posthumous attack on the Emperor, he made a serious start. When he left Milan he left the manuscript with his friend Luigi Buzzi, and there it remained until, after his death, Mareste brought it back and gave it to Colomb. Now, in November, 1836, he began a completely new work, making use of Las Cases and the other books and documents newly available. He worked on it for five or six months, until the following April: after this, at intervals for a year or so he made notes, not a great many, before giving it up, in effect for good. There is a letter in Mérimée's collected correspondence, written 12 February 1837, commenting severely on a part of the manuscript he has seen, part of a preface; he found it completely without method or solidity, the ill sewn together work of an amateur scholar. Mérimée, who never undertook anything at which he was only an amateur, no doubt knew what he was talking about. But if all Stendhal's research for his unfinished task enriched by only a detail or two the enchanting account of Fabrice at Waterloo and the pages on the joyous entry of the young revolutionary French army into Milan on 15 May 1796 it had not been a waste of time.

In Rome he had laid hands—in a bookshop or a library, possibly in the archives of the ancient and distinguished Caetani family, in whose sixteenth-century palazzo he was a frequent guest—on a number of Italian manuscripts of the sixteenth and seventeenth centuries. Delighted by the violence and energy of the incidents recorded in them he bought some and had others copied for him; twelve, he says: in fact, at the time of his death, he possessed fourteen. He planned to write a series of *nouvelles* based on them and proposed to Buloz, the director of the *Revue des deux mondes*, to give him six or seven, and did give him four: *Vittoria Accoramboni*, published anonymously in March 1837, and *Les Cenci*, written in May and June and published 1 July: at the same time, between April and June, he was at work on a never completed novel (*Rose et Vert*), and the following year, within a few days of getting back to Paris from the longest and most demanding of his journeys for the *Mémoires d'un Touriste* he began to dictate the *Duchesse de Palliano*. All three shock by their frenetic brilliance as much as by their cruelty. They could be the work of a Webster in control of his imagination, and were the work of a connoisseur of human nature fascinated by the spectacle of well-born men and women behaving without any of the restraints imposed by moral sentiments. Reckless energy in a man or woman

drew from him an involuntary response, something like a re-
pudiation, without any conceivable issue in act, of his own deep
sensitivity: such men and women were free, as he could not be.
Julien Sorel is not the only character in his novels who is both
heroic, to be admired and liked, and capable of savagery in
thought and deed.

He had been seduced from his Napoleonic effort by the idea of
writing a book on travel in France. Nothing else in his life came
so close to the intense pleasure music gave him as the delight he
got out of travel. Out of the simplest travel; out of evenings spent
talking with his table companions in the inn or the hotel—'un
hotel *snog*'—of a provincial town he arrived in as an anonymous
stranger and lived in for two days, a week, walking about its
streets, visiting its market, churches, bookshops, museums,
picture galleries, curiosities, monuments, ruins, every sense alert,
delighted to be unknown and free. On the road the view of a
distant line of hills, a lake, sun-warm mountain slopes, seen from
the window of the coach, lifted him to a level of contentment
which withstood even moments of boredom: this lover of mountains found the banks of the Loire dull. His own contentment, his
endless pleasure in details—the brilliance of a sky, the outline of a
face, the scent of thyme and wild lavender in the bare country of
the Pont du Gard—explain, a little, the lasting fascination of the
Mémoires d'un Touriste. One or other of my copies went with me on
every journey through France for years: it is the easiest travel book
in the world to read. Its perenniality springs from Stendhal's unwearying curiosity about human beings, a curiosity at once
intellectual and sensuous, their manners and customs, commerce,
politics, history, opinions, prejudices, follies, starting in him a
torrent of original speculations, never more lucid and endearing
than when completely arbitrary. He took immense pains to
prepare himself for his journeys, reading widely and again laying
friends and acquaintances under contribution, descriptions of
Nîmes and Marseille from Mareste, interminable dull accounts of
Gauls and lesser races from the learned Dr Edwards (to whose un-
fashionable salon he had been faithful out of respect for its

simplicity) which, alas, he quotes in full, archaeology from Mérimée. During brief journeys they made together in the provinces the authoritative Inspector of Historic Monuments tried with very mild success to teach him something about ecclesiastical architecture. 'Beyle m'a toujours paru assez indifférent à l'architecture,' he observes drily in his *H.B.* 'Je crois lui avoir appris à distinguer une église romane d'une église gothique, et, qui plus est, à regarder l'une et l'autre.' He could not infect Beyle with his own passionate care for old neglected churches in France. Beyle found them devoid of the sensuous pleasure he looked for in architecture as in music; he infinitely preferred the gaiety and elegance of the Italian Renaissance.

He cannot have begun the actual writing before July 1837 when he came back from Brittany, and on 4 January he was correcting the first pages of the proofs. He was already travelling for a third volume when the two others came out; and the lukewarm reception they were given disappointed him. He had left Paris early in March, for Angoulême and Bordeaux, the first stages of a journey which lasted nearly five months and, for all his love of the Midi, exhausted him. In June he was in Grenoble for the last time. If he made notes there of his impressions, reveries, regrets, they are lost, with all else he may, must, have recorded of the last two months of this journey. There remains from this time a handful of pages he wrote down during a magnificently moonlit evening near Montpellier, on his way from Narbonne to Marseille, and intended—surely?—to include in the new volume. But, no, one cannot be sure of anything except of the slightly sceptical smile of amusement with which he glanced back to himself: 'Autrefois, dès que j'étais seul, je rêvais à des aventures d'amour tendres et romanesques. . . . J'étais bien plus fou, mais bien plus heureux quand, sans en rien dire à personne, et déjà grand garçon et donnant des signatures officielles, je songeais toujours aux plaisirs que me croyait à la vielle d'éprouver . . . je voudrais presque redevenir une dupe et un nigaud dans la réalité de la vie, et reprendre les charmantes rêveries si absurdes qui me donnaient des soirées si charmantes. . . .'

It is for the very rare moments when, calmly aware of his failures and vulnerability, without indulgence for himself, he dropped the mask, that we love him.

From Grenoble he went by stages to Geneva and Strasbourg and came home through Cologne, Rotterdam, Amsterdam, Antwerp, Brussels, to reach Paris in the last weeks of July. Almost at once he began work on the *Duchesse de Palliano*, and Buloz published it on 15 August. Did he then go to London, as only Romain Colomb says he did, and visit the Athenæum, taken there by Sutton Sharpe? If he did, it was the last time he saw his friend: Sharpe died, of overwork and his mode of life, only eleven months after Beyle himself. What is certain is that in August he looked through his Italian chronicles and was caught again—he had read it earlier—by the splendidly scandalous story of Vanezza Farnèse, a Borgia's mistress, and her young nephew, that dissolute Alexandre Farnèse who became Pope Paul III. At some moment during the next three weeks he was invaded by the idea of transposing the action of the story to the Napoleonic epoch in Italy and opening it with an account of Waterloo. He may have drafted it first as a *nouvelle*, and when its superb possibilities as a novel seized him he did not immediately set to work: an epiphany, the right word in this context, demands, even from a great writer or especially from a great writer, a pause like the pause before the conductor's baton is raised: with the soundest of instincts he left the theme where it was safe—in his mind—and went off on a journey that took him from Orléans to Nantes, Rennes, Avranches, Bayeux, Caen, Honfleur, Rouen. Back in Paris at the beginning of November he gave orders to his concierge that visitors were to be told that he was absent, shut himself in his room, and in a single jet of imaginative power between 4 November and 26 December, fifty-two days, he wrote and dictated, and dictated and wrote, the whole of the *Chartreuse de Parme*, a long densely intricate narrative drawn from the richest veins of his experience and reflections and conducted with seemingly effortless though feverish energy, and offering, in Mosca, one of his greatest creations.

More nearly than any other of his works it approached the

condition of music, of the music he preferred: in its wit, gaiety, tenderness, underlying tension and sadness, it is the most Mozartian of his novels, even to the speed with which it was composed. This book is not haunted by the myth of Napoleon, as was *Le Rouge et le Noir*: after the magnificent overture it scarcely reappears: he had nothing fresh to say. Inevitably the single great love of Fabrice's life, for the gentle-hearted Clélia, stirs the ghost of a Métilde whose lover never, except in 'the enchanting reveries of crystallisation', heard from her the words Clélia speaks when she opens the door of a darkened room—'Entre ici, ami de mon cœur.' The end, a dangerously impulsive Sanseverina grown old, Clélia dead, her child, Fabrice's son, dead, Fabrice spending the last year of a short recklessly uncalculating life in the solitude of a Carthusian cell, has the exquisite finality of *Don Giovanni*: the sadness, the defeat, are endurable because what above all remains in the reader's mind is Stendhal's overwhelming pleasure in writing this one of his books. The day is ending, but the light is that of his setting-out.

Chapter 11

HE HAD NEVER been able simply to rest. 'Allez à la chasse de bonheur' is a purely Stendhalian phrase; it covers every form in which he used his energy. Now, in the short interval of freedom he had left, he not only revised the proofs of his novel, but wrote for Buloz the splendid *Abbesse de Castro* and began and left unfinished four other works. His time in Paris was up. He left in June, and with halts in Zurich, Lucerne, Genoa, Leghorn, Sienna, made the journey to Civitavecchia last seven weeks. His insouciance did him no harm in Rome. During his prolonged leave the French ambassador had died and been succeeded by his brother, and not only was the Comte Septime de la Tour-Maubourg as willing to handle him gently, but there was a degree of cousinage involved, in that his first wife had been a Daru, a daughter of Alexandrine Daru. When Henri Beyle dined or attended a ball at the embassy he did so as a member of the family.

He took up his duties again with resolution. There is nothing surprising in his competence in a task he disliked and neglected when he comfortably could; he had a head for administration, and the respect for rules of procedure of his Gagnon forebears; and but for the flaw in his nature, the flaw which produced *Le Rouge et le Noir* and the *Chartreuse de Parme*, he could hardly have failed to establish himself at least as well as, let us say, Thiers. A consul *malgré lui*, he was an authoritative one.

As soon as he had settled back into his consular office he took up again a novel for which, before leaving Paris, he had made a quantity of notes. Critics have seen *Lamiel* as an attempt at a portrait in depth of a young woman determined to use the rights of a man, a female Julien Sorel without his reasoned duplicity. She is more a handsome untamed boy with the energies and passions of an unscrupulous adventurer, and in the only completed part of the novel she exists as a series of gestures, intimations of a figure still three-quarters fast in the clay. One doubts whether under any circumstances Stendhal would have made his way to the end he projected, Lamiel's death in setting fire to the Palais de Justice to avenge her assassin lover. What defeated him? More than any technical difficulty, the incoherence of the theme; it had no roots in the philosophy, the experience, the exultations and agonies of his life. Driven to invent both action and characters, he was again and again baffled, and in the end bored.

In October Mérimée arrived in Italy from Corsica. He spent ten days with Beyle in Rome and three weeks in Naples, visiting Paestum, Pompeii, and Herculaneum. Something, some friction, developed between them during this time—or was it simply that a month spent together was too long, long enough for each to realise acutely that they no longer shared the same intellectual habits and creeds? Henri Beyle had not changed except physically; Mérimée had: he had gone a long way towards realising the energies and ambitions apparent, though not then to Beyle, in the young man he met when Mérimée was eighteen. The serious scholar, the immensely knowledgeable and hardworking Inspector of Historic Monuments he had become, valued and well-liked by his ministers, by the royal family, by a great many distinguished men and women, was not and never had been malicious or insensitive. He had real kindness, natural wit, integrity, and with them a highly critical commonsense: whatever his sympathy for Beyle he can hardly have escaped a certain involuntary contempt for what looked like a series of failures, disappointments, and above all, errors of judgement. At this meeting Beyle irritated him by lecturing him on historical Rome. Writing from Rome on 15 October 1839 to his friend Esprit Requien, curator of the local museum of Avignon, rich, erudite, with a ribald wit, he told him: 'Je ne comptais pas voir Rome et je me suis laissé entrainer par M. Beyle. J'en suis on ne peut pas plus content. Je dis de Rome.' And no doubt he put Beyle in his place as classicist and amateur archaeologist: in one of his innumerable marginal notes Beyle recorded that 'the frightful vanity of Academus ruined this trip to Naples'. Mérimée had become *académisable*—it twitched the nerve of irony in Beyle, and the more sharply that he was not without academic ambitions himself, with no reasonable likelihood of achieving them.

The two once close friends met again, in Paris, three months before Beyle died. His death did not wrench Mérimée as did Sutton Sharpe's less than a year later. That hurt him very very deeply: he could not get used to Sharpe's absence, nor forgive himself for not going to London to see him in his last illness. Beyle's disappearance he took with commendable calm. At first he intended to write about him in the *Revue des deux Mondes*. But he knew next to nothing about his life before they met, and not a great deal about his work, and failed to get either details or anecdotes from Mareste to whom he wrote asking for them on the same day as he wrote to Romain Colomb to ask where Beyle had been born and for the basic details of his life and the dates and titles of his books. Colomb made it politely clear that what he expected from Mérimée was a study of the writer, not a biographical account. In fact Mérimée had no very high opinion of Stendhal's writings: he dropped the idea of providing an obituary essay, and refused coldly to commend Colomb's own essay to Buloz, damning it as mediocre. It was years later, when he had suffered and was tired, that he turned and looked back to his friend with a gentle pity. In December 1853, the first collected edition of Stendhal's work, nineteen volumes, put together with the greatest care and sublime devotion by Colomb, was on the verge of publication; and Sainte-Beuve, meditating an essay on the occasion, wanted to discuss it with Mérimée. 'Veuillez m'écrire,' Mérimée wrote him, 'seulement quand vous voulez que nous conférions ensemble de ce pauvre garçon qui était bien meilleur qu'il ne le laissait paraître' . . . this poor fellow who was infinitely better than he let himself seem. . . . It may be a faint touch too kindly, but it moves.

To all appearances the life Beyle returned to in Rome and

Civitavecchia was in every way the one he had fled from three years earlier. He was almost as often in Rome as in his consulate, staying at Castelgandolfo with the Cini family; meeting and gossiping with the two younger Caetanis; present, having taken very great care with his dress, wig, and close-cut line of dyed beard, at all grand occasions. He had a new lodging, in the house of an art dealer, a room on the second floor, cheap and very near the Corso; not so near Abraham Constantin, whom none the less he met most days and talked and drank coffee with him in the café del Greco. Now and then he went farther afield than Albano; he was in Florence twice, for twenty days. In Civitavecchia he had moved from his room overlooking harbour and ramparts to a new pleasant apartment with four rooms and his friend Donato Bucci as neighbour: the sea in the evening, a wide fleece of light, drew him; he watched it for hours. His only other amusement here, apart from visits to the latest excavations, was lark shooting in the country behind the little town. Much the same life: the change was in Beyle, in his thickened body, hardly at all in his mind.

In the first February after he came back his unappeased heart led him into a brief, very brief and frustrate incident of which nothing remains except scattered notes in his indecipherable writing, and a name—Earline. Nothing else—an emptiness. It was formless and illusory from the start, a last unanswered demand for a love no woman living could have given him.

He was at Civitavecchia when the mid-October boat delivered to him the copy of the *Revue parisienne* with Balzac's seventy-page long review of the *Chartreuse de Parme*. He was half surprised, half enormously pleased: his pleasure gives away an unspoken disappointment in the meagreness of his recognition as a writer, a disappointment he very rarely allowed himself to feel; he could the more easily ignore it because, very early, he taught himself—or was born not needing this particular lesson—to look at himself and his work without either complacence or modesty. He kept his secrets. Nevertheless he felt a sense of warmth and triumph rise through him. He thought it over for two days, then drafted his reply rapidly: discontented with it, he made a second and a third long draft—grateful, frank, defending himself delicately against Balzac's criticism of his style, explaining himself, even agreeing that he would delete or amend passages, which, praise be, he mercifully failed to do, and the *Chartreuse* remains as he wrote it, a union of sensuousness and technical control from which it would be difficult without loss to erase a stroke.

His health was worsening. Since his return he had had frequent violent headaches, migraine, and attacks of vertigo, with other ills: there can be little doubt that the syphilis—if it was syphilis—he contracted in Milan in 1800 had worked stealthily in him ever since: he was several times treated with mercury, notably in Vienna.

He was seriously stricken in Civitavecchia in March: face to face with *le néant*, he told Domenico di Fiore, asking him not to tell Colomb; he wanted it kept quiet. He struggled through, tried to work on *Lamiel*, making only amendments, and wrote at least one official letter to Guizot, now Foreign Minister. From Rome, where he had gone at the end of the month to consult doctors—these included the Pope's own doctor—he wrote to di Fiore again, on the 10th of April: 'Je trouve qu'il n'y a pas de ridicule à mourir dans la rue, quand on ne le fait pas exprès.' He became desperately ill here, an apoplectic assault: the treatment was as savage as the disease, but at the end of May Guizot received a long letter from him about the shipping in and out of Civitavecchia, and in June and July he was flooding the Paris office with details of the commercial transactions of the government in Rome.

Early in August that year a young painter, Henri Lehmann, a naturalised Frenchman, came to Civitavecchia. The pencil drawing he made of the consul—not in uniform—is the last portrait we have of him, and except in the trace of mockery on the fine-lipped mouth it is unlike any other; a smiling mockery, a mocking kindness: the other features, the narrowed eyes, a certain stiffness, are those of a heavily ageing man; only the smile offers a vague glimpse of the lively loving child he was born.

This month he asked Guizot for sick leave; he was told he could take it when Lysimaque Tavernier, who was in Constantinople being married, had returned. He waited. In October he had five days in Rome, exquisite days of a Roman autumn.

Lysimaque had added to his other iniquities the crowning insolence of getting the cross of the Légion d'honneur, and one of Henri Beyle's last duties in the month before he left was to pin it on him.

He left on 22 October. From Marseille he went directly to Geneva, to consult the distinguished Dr Prévost, who had looked after him, his gout, his attack of stone, in the past, and in whom, more now as a friend, he believed: if anyone could help him, it was the Genevan. He was so exhausted that it was another week before he could face the three-day coach journey to Paris.

He recovered during the winter, enough to be able to amuse himself: music, Rossini's *Barber*, the theatre, suppers with friends. Many of the salons he had known were gone. By a happy irony his pleasantest evenings this winter were spent in a house where in 1828 he had started badly: Mme Ancelot was a vivacious and possibly designing hostess to academicians and such, and having got themselves invited to her Tuesdays it had amused Beyle and a young Mérimée to make none too subtle fun of her: the quietly dignified letter she wrote Beyle, protesting, shamed him, if not into curbing his tongue, into respect and liking. The *Monsieur et ami* with which she begins her letters to him now, in 1841, and the *tendre et sincère attachment* on which they close measure exactly her genuine affection for him and the distance of their relations. She set herself this winter to cherish him. I daresay that when she urged him to offer himself as candidate for the Academy and promised her help, she was at once sincere and doubtful that he would like to make the attempt. That he took the idea seriously, talking to Colomb about it, is—a little sorrowful.

His doctors had forbidden him to attempt to write. But early in March he was feeling stronger than he had felt for a long time, and he started working; and worked as he had been used to, all day, in a fever of energy: a revised chapter of *Lamiel*, notes for a series of *nouvelles*. On the 21st of March he signed a contract for two of these with the *Revue des deux mondes*. The following day he had been working very hard when, in the evening, he set out to walk down the rue Neuve-des-Capucines. Struck down by an attack of apoplexy, he was carried into a shop, then to his lodging in the hôtel de Nantes, rue Neuve-des-Petits-Champs, and died, still unconscious, at two in the morning.

It was the sudden death without moral or physical pain he once said he wanted. For the Enrico Beyle, Milanese, lover of Cimarosa, Mozart and Shakespeare, of the epitaph he had written for himself twenty-two years earlier, in Milan, in 1820, death at the right time, but it came sooner than he wanted.

Early in his life Henri Beyle had concluded that happiness is a state of grace to be reached in one way only: by forming the habit of not lying to himself about his own actions and motives, and by putting himself to school with the greatest minds of past and present. He had no one he trusted to tell him how to proceed. His self-imposed duty was to look at himself, at this animal which thinks and feels, without complacence, and to sharpen his intellect into an instrument for probing the minds and motives of other men. In December 1801—that is, in his eighteenth year—he noted in his Journal: 'Presque tous les malheurs de la vie viennent des fausses idées que nous avons sur ce qui nous arrive. Connaître à fond les hommes, juger sainement des événements, est donc un grand pas vers le bonheur.' And towards becoming a great poet. The only surprising thing about this double conclusion is not that he came to it so nearly at the beginning of his rational life, but that he carried it through. He fell into every sort of error, devoured every fragment of experience which came his way, and, so far as anyone could, looked at himself with naked honesty. Others he duped, not himself.

Possibly all his friends, not only Mérimée, for one reason or another, in one sense or another, felt that he had bungled his life. What nonsense! From the child born with a genius for happiness, an uncommon sensitivity, and a divine gaiety, to the gouty consul enjoying the cool of the day in a modest café in Rome, his life was triumphant, its every moment a refusal of defeat. Hence the love, the complicity, we feel for him. Hence the incomparable pleasure of returning again and again to books which have the grace and suppleness of young athletes stripped to run a race.

A man, said Valéry, with whom we shall never have done. The writers of whom this can be said, are, on calm reflection, few.

Short Reading List

Alain (Émile-Auguste Chartier). *Stendhal* (Collection Maîtres des Littératures). Paris: Rieder, 1935

Bardèche, Maurice. *Stendhal romancier.* Paris: Éditions de la Table Ronde, 1947

Green, F. C. *Stendhal.* Cambridge University Press, 1939

Hemmings, F. W. J. *Stendhal. A Study of his Novels.* Oxford: Clarendon Press, 1964

Martineau, Henri. *Le Cœur de Stendhal* (2 vols). Paris: Éditions Albin Michel, 1952

Prévost, Jean. *La création chez Stendhal.* Paris: Mercure de France, 1951

Thibaudet, Albert. *Stendhal.* Paris: Hachette, 1931

Turnell, Martin. *The Novel in France* (pp. 125–208). London: Hamish Hamilton, 1950

STENDHAL'S WORKS

Short list: essential reading

Vie de Henry Brulard (2 vols)
La Chartreuse de Parme
Le Rouge et le Noir
Lucien Leuwen
Souvenirs d'Égotisme
Armance, ou quelques scènes d'un salon de Paris en 1827
De l'amour
Mémoires d'un Touriste
Correspondance—Pléiades edition (3 vols)

Index

157